Psychology Licensure
and Certification

Psychology Licensure and Certification

What Students Need to Know

Edited by **Thomas J. Vaughn**

American Psychological Association • Washington, DC

Published by
American Psychological Association
750 First Street, NE
Washington, DC 20002
www.apa.org

To order
APA Order Department
P.O. Box 92984
Washington, DC 20090-2984
Tel: (800) 374-2721; Direct: (202) 336-5510
Fax: (202) 336-5502; TDD/TTY: (202) 336-6123
Online: www.apa.org/books/
E-mail: order@apa.org

In the U.K., Europe, Africa, and the Middle East, copies may be ordered from
American Psychological Association
3 Henrietta Street
Covent Garden, London
WC2E 8LU England

Typeset in Meridien by World Composition Services, Inc., Sterling, VA

Printer: Victor Graphics, Baltimore, MD
Cover Designer: Naylor Design, Washington, DC
Technical/Production Editor: Tiffany L. Klaff

The opinions and statements published are the responsibility of the authors, and such opinions and statements do not necessarily represent the policies of the American Psychological Association.

Library of Congress Cataloging-in-Publication Data

Psychology licensure and certification : what students need to know /
[edited by] Thomas J. Vaughn. — 1st ed.
   p. cm.
   ISBN 1-59147-407-8
   1. Psychologists—Certification—United States. 2. Psychologists
—Licenses—United States. 3. Psychologists—Certification—Canada.
4. Psychologists—Licenses—Canada. I. Vaughn, Thomas J.

BF80.8.P78 2006
150.23'73—dc22
                                                        2005036422

British Library Cataloguing-in-Publication Data
A CIP record is available from the British Library.

Printed in the United States of America
First Edition

Contents

Contributors

Judith S. Blanton, PhD, ABPP, Managing Director, RHR International Company, Los Angeles, CA

Patricia M. Bricklin, PhD, former President, Association of State and Provincial Psychology Boards; Professor, Widener University, Chester, PA

Janet Ciuccio, MA, Assistant Executive Director, New Business and Constituent Operations, American Psychological Association Practice Organization, Washington, DC

Patrick H. DeLeon, PhD, JD, ABPP, former President, American Psychological Association, Washington, DC

Stephen T. DeMers, EdD, Executive Officer and Former President, Association of State and Provincial Psychology Boards, Montgomery, AL

Melanie M. Echols, PhD, private practice, Lifespan Psychological Services, Atlanta, GA

Raymond D. Fowler, PhD, San Diego State University, San Diego, CA

Ronald E. Fox, PhD, ABPP, former President, American Psychological Association; The Consulting Group of HRC, Chapel Hill, NC

Gerald K. Gentry, PhD, former President, Association of State and Provincial Psychology Boards; private practice, Olathe, KS

Judy E. Hall, PhD, former President, Association of State and Provincial Psychology Boards; Executive Officer, National Register of Health Service Providers in Psychology, Washington, DC

Billie J. Hinnefeld, JD, PhD, Senior Director, Legal and Regulatory Affairs, American Psychological Association, Washington, DC

Kim R. Jonason, PhD, former President, Association of State and Provincial Psychology Boards; private practice, Louisville, KY

Nadine J. Kaslow, PhD, ABPP, former President, Association of Psychology Postdoctoral and Internship Centers; Professor and Chief Psychologist, Department of Psychiatry and Behavioral Sciences, Emory University, Atlanta, GA

W. Greg Keilin, PhD, Past President, Association of Psychology Postdoctoral and Internship Centers; Assistant Director, Counseling and Mental Health Center, University of Texas, Austin

Robert H. Lipkins, PhD, Senior Program Director, Professional Examination Service, New York, NY

William T. Melnyk, PhD, former President, Association of State and Provincial Psychology Boards; Professor, Department of Psychology, Lakehead University, Murillo, Ontario, Canada

Russell S. Newman, PhD, JD, Executive Director, American Psychological Association Practice Organization, Washington, DC

Ted Packard, PhD, ABPP, former President, Association of State and Provincial Psychology Boards and American Board of Professional Psychology; Professor, Department of Educational Psychology, University of Utah, Salt Lake City

Randolph P. Reaves, JD, Randolph P. Reaves, PC, Attorney, Montgomery, AL

Lynn P. Rehm, PhD, ABPP, past Chair, Examination Committee, Association of State and Provincial Psychology Boards; Professor, Department of Psychology, University of Houston, Houston, TX

Pierre L. J. Ritchie, PhD, Executive Director, Canadian Register of Health Service Providers in Psychology; Professor, University of Ottawa, Ottawa, Ontario, Canada

Emil R. Rodolfa, PhD, former President, Association of Psychology Postdoctoral and Internship Centers; Director, Counseling and Psychological Services, University of California, Davis

Norma P. Simon, PhD, ABPP, former President, Association of State and Provincial Psychology Boards; President, American Board of Professional Psychology; private practice, New York, NY

L. Craig Turner, PhD, President, Canadian Register of Health Service Providers in Psychology; private practice, Winnipeg, Manitoba, Canada

Barbara A. Van Horne, MBA, PhD, Director of Professional Affairs and Former President, Association of State and Provincial Psychology Boards, Montgomery, AL

Karen S. Vaughn, MA, former Director of Communications and Technology, Association of State and Provincial Psychology Boards; University of Oklahoma, Norman

Thomas J. Vaughn, PhD, ABPP, former President, Association of State and Provincial Psychology Boards; private practice, Behavioral Medicine Associates, Shawnee, OK

Erica H. Wise, PhD, Vice Chair, National Register of Health Service Providers in Psychology; Director, Psychology Clinic and Clinical Associate Professor, Department of Psychology, University of North Carolina, Chapel Hill

Psychology Licensure
and Certification

Thomas J. Vaughn

Introduction

Following the Credentials Committee review of your application, the Board of Examiners of Psychologists regrets to inform you that you do not qualify under the law for licensure as a psychologist in this jurisdiction. The Board has determined that even though your program was accredited by the American Psychological Association (APA), your transcript as verified by the registrar of your university does not contain all of the coursework required for licensure, that is, ethics and standards. In addition to other deficiencies, your APA-accredited internship at Central Counseling Center was for 1,520 hours, was completed in 46 weeks, had only one licensed psychologist supervisor, and provided only 128 hours of supervision. Although the Board has on an individual basis allowed the remediation of a course, your internship is so problematic as to require the completion of a fully integrated internship that would meet our licensure requirements. If in the future you believe that you have completed all of the requirements for licensure, we will be pleased to receive another application.

One of the primary purposes of this book is to prevent students from receiving this letter. The book is designed to provide students and their faculty with difficult-to-locate information concerning licensure and certification in psychology, with the goal that every student will qualify for licensure in any state or province in which they have an interest to practice.

Chapter authors are authorities in their topic areas, including history, doctoral program, internship, postdoctoral experience, examinations, mobility, national credentialing, board certification and specialization, extended competencies, ethics and standards, and indicators of the future directions of practice for both health service psychologists and non-health service psychologists. The book provides students and faculty with a total range of resources that can be used to answer questions definitively. Questions regarding qualifications for licensure are covered in chapter 1 as an overview of standard licensure requirements across states and provinces. This chapter also includes discussion of pitfalls in education and supervised experience that can lead to licensure problems. How licensure developed and why the licensure requirements that are common to the profession are currently in place are covered in chapter 2. The considerable resources available from the Association of State and Provincial Psychology Boards (ASPPB), the members of which are all of the licensing boards in the United States and Canada, is the subject of the chapter 3. Of special interest is the *Handbook of Licensing and Certification Requirements* that is available online for free at http://www.asppb.org/handbook/handbook.aspx.[1]

Perhaps the most anxiety-producing subject of "examinations" is covered in chapters 4 and 5. The Examination for Professional Practice in Psychology and the jurisprudence and oral examinations used by licensing boards are discussed in detail.

Questions about predoctoral internships and the postdoctoral year of supervision are covered in chapters 6 and 7 together with practical information for students who are seeking placements.

Questions regarding the need for professional mobility and the importance of the development of the ASPPB Student Credentials Bank, and its Certificate of Professional Qualification in Psychology, and the National Register of Health Service Providers in Psychology Student Register are addressed in chapters 8, 9, and 11.

The growing need and both internal (profession) and external (hospital staffs and third-party payers) expectations for psychologists to move beyond generic licensure and become board certified in a specialty by the American Board of Professional Psychology is presented well in chapter 10.

The need for psychologists to be able to illustrate a proficiency in specific professional skills and treatments through the APA College of Professional Psychology is covered in chapter 12. Examinations are

---

[1] Association of State and Provincial Psychology Boards. (2005). *Handbook of licensing and certification requirements*. Retrieved January 18, 2006, from http://www.asppb.org/handbook/handbook.aspx

available to establish proficiencies in alcohol and substance abuse treatment, and psychopharmacology.

Special licensure and certification issues for non-health service psychologists, especially those who practice in industrial/organizational and business consulting psychology are discussed in chapter 13.

Postgraduate preparation for obtaining prescriptive authority is the subject of chapter 14. As the state and provincial licensing laws change to provide an extension of the scope of practice for psychologists to prescribe psychoactive medications as a part of their treatment, this proficiency will become more important for students entering the profession.

Ethics and standards of practice and professional codes of conduct, together with specific recommendations for handling common conflicts and problems in professional practice, and some dos and don'ts make chapter 15 a must for providing good practice and staying out of trouble.

The capstone of what psychologists might expect with regard to future trends in practice is presented in chapter 16. Bravely, I might add.

Finally, in the appendixes a myriad of confusing acronyms are revealed, and a list of useful Web sites and forms for recording coursework, internship, and postdoctoral experience are provided.

This book offers information that will enable you to take care of yourself, and to ask questions of those who present you with a program of study that may very well place you in many tens of thousands of dollars in debt; debt that you will be responsible for repaying. So ask questions.

Will this program enable you to be licensed in every state or province where you may wish to practice? What is the ratio of students admitted to the program to actual doctoral graduates? What is the percentage of graduates that become licensed as psychologists? What is the student to faculty ratio? What is the percentage of full-time faculty to part-time faculty? What is the quality of practicum experience offered and does the program provide placements or are you left to scramble up something on your own? What is the specific expertise of faculty members to teach the courses that they teach? How much face-to-face time will you have with each of your teachers? How much face-to-face time will you have with your major advisor? What is the quality of internships that graduates were accepted into, and how many went to APA- or CPA-accredited internships? Is this a distance education program that is being described with some other more acceptable label? What level of financial support in the form of grants and assistantships does the program provide? How anxious is the program to provide you with their access to loans? What is the percentage of graduates that are employed immediately following receipt of their doctorate, what percentage are employed as psychologists, and what is the average length of time it took for their graduates to become employed as psychologists? Is this program interested in your professional and financial future or theirs?

Trainers and supervisors in quality programs should be well aware of these issues and able to provide you with more than satisfactory answers. Pay attention to whether they blink, divert, stumble, take offense, or avoid when you ask these questions. There is a reason for that. I hope that I have raised just enough concern that you will ask these questions before they become critical in your doctoral training. Read on as we present what students need to know to prepare for entry into the most interesting and rewarding of all professions.

Thomas J. Vaughn

Overview of Licensure Requirements to Meet "High Standard" in the United States and Canada

1

Although the history of licensure is well chronicled in other chapters of this book, it is important for students to understand that licensure has been established by the legislative bodies of each jurisdiction (U.S. state or Canadian province) for the purpose of protecting the public, not the profession (Hess, 1977). In enacting licensure for professionals, legislative bodies established requirements for the title and usually for the scope of practice of the professions they have chosen to regulate. The public can be assured that any person licensed in a profession has met the requirements of education, supervised experience, and independent examination required by law and is therefore entitled to publicly claim the title and practice the profession within the state or province. Unless specifically exempted from the law, a person who does not meet these requirements cannot legally refer to him- or herself as being a member of the profession, use the title, or practice in any area defined as within the scope of practice of the profession (Meyer & Altmaier, 1985; Wiens, 1983; Wiens & Dorken, 1986). Charlatans cannot and will not be licensed. Through this vehicle of professional licensure, the legislative bodies do no less than warranty the public trust.

Licensure laws are generic. As such, all of the requirements for obtaining a license in psychology pertain to all areas of psychology, be they practice, academic, or consulting. All applicants for licensure must meet the same core requirements for education, supervised experience, and examination. In the past, there has been tremendous variance in these requirements; however, the Association of State and Provincial Psychology Boards (ASPPB) has for many years attempted to help their member psychology licensing boards move toward more standard licensing laws and rules. Crucial to this endeavor, ASPPB established a standardized written examination for psychology licensure. All U.S. states, and all but one Canadian province, use the Examination for Professional Practice in Psychology (EPPP), and finally, all use the same passing score (ASPPB, 2005a).

It is imperative that all graduate students or prospective graduate students understand and accept that it is ultimately their personal responsibility to ensure that they meet all of the requirements for licensure as a psychologist. The primary tragic circumstance occurs when students complete their program, internship, and postdoctoral experience only to find that they are not licensable in the state or province where they had hoped or planned to practice. The secondary tragic circumstance occurs after students have received their first license and seek to move to accept a new position and learn that because of deficiencies in their training and supervised experience required by the new jurisdiction, they are not licensable (Jonason, DeMers, Vaughn, & Reaves, 2003; Vaughn, 1993). In either case, a career is limited by a lack of attention to a foreseeable defect in their preparation.

I hope that most who are reading this book are undergraduates who are considering a graduate program, or at least are 1st or 2nd year graduate students. For those who are in an American Psychological Association (APA) or Canadian Psychological Association (CPA) accredited program in a Health Service Psychologist (HSP) area (clinical, counseling, or school) their program has illustrated to APA or CPA that the program has met the criteria established by these bodies for accreditation (APA, 2005c). Note that the emphasis is on the program, not on any student within the program. Individual students may or may not have met the curriculum requirements that the accreditation status of the program would seem to indicate. Therefore, psychology licensing boards have been advised by accreditation bodies to attend to the transcript of the individual applicant rather than continuing, as in the past, to rely on the accreditation status of their program in determining the applicant's legal qualification for licensure within the jurisdiction (Hargrove, 2003). For those who are in non-HSP areas that are not accredited by APA or CPA (industrial/organizational [I/O], experimental, developmental, educational, etc.), note especially the generic licensure requirements following (and see chap.13, this volume, about I/O non-HSP).

The term *high standard* has been chosen for use in this chapter as representative of the more stringent level in the combination of licensure requirements that are common to most jurisdictions in the United States and Canada. Some jurisdictions will require less, and others more, in each of the licensure requirement areas described; however, those students who meet these high standard requirements will be eligible to sit for licensure in most jurisdictions with little or no remediation. If the student's program, internship, and postdoctoral supervision placements do not ensure that these minimums are met, then the student must see to it that they are met on their own. The ASPPB (2005c) has published the *Handbook of Licensing and Certification Requirements* that includes the major licensing requirements of every ASPPB member jurisdiction in the United States and Canada (http://www.asppb.org/handbook/handbook.aspx). Students should use this extremely valuable online resource to check the licensure requirements of jurisdictions where they may be interested in obtaining a license. Regardless of the quality or completeness of the program's records, students should keep a written record of everything. Because of the thorough specificity required by most licensing boards, the best form available for recording your program coursework, internship, and postdoctoral experience is found in the "Information for Students" section of the ASPPB Web site, with an abbreviated version in Appendix C of this book (also see chap. 9, this volume).

The Graduate Program

When considering a graduate program in psychology, students in HSP areas are well advised to limit their consideration to only those programs that are APA- or CPA-accredited (APA, 2005a; CPA, 2005). This offers some, albeit limited, protection for licensure qualification in the future. These programs are housed in institutions that are regionally accredited by the U.S. Department of Education, or in the case of Canada, authorized by provincial statute or Royal Charter. The doctoral program, even those that are not APA or CPA accredited, should be designed to meet all APA or CPA criteria for accreditation. Although there is variation in degree and specificity, licensing laws (most of which are based on APA and ASPPB model licensure acts) do contain elements of these standards in their educational requirements.

Beware, as there are still U.S. programs housed in institutions that are only state accredited (not regionally accredited), and a degree from one of these institutions will not meet the licensure requirements in any other jurisdiction (Vaughn, 1999; Waters, 2000).

Also beware of the term *equivalent* when used by programs to describe anything related to accreditation or licensure. *Equivalent* means "not actually." The use of Internet instruction is a growing and valuable ancillary tool of professional instruction in many university and professional psychology graduate programs. The use of this individual or virtual online group instruction is likely to increase in the future, and if the professional and legislative communities embrace this change as in the best interest of the public, then it is possible that licensure laws will be changed to accommodate these realities. Although some professionals and some legislators advocate the use of distance learning as an "equivalent" substitute for on-campus instruction, at the present time this view is espoused by few of either. This may change; however at the present time, only students who have a high degree of tolerance for scrutiny of their credentials, and rejection of same, should consider a program that uses distance learning as the primary methodology of instruction. Students enrolling in these "schools without walls" must be aware that such programs are not likely to meet the course, supervised practicum, or 1- to 2-year full-time residency requirements for licensure in other jurisdictions. Gathering students for a weekend, or for a month here and there, is not the professional training or legal equivalent of a full-time year on campus. As a result, students entering these programs are at serious risk for having limited career opportunities.

In addition to the APA and ASPPB Model Licensure Acts, ASPPB and the National Register of Health Service Providers in Psychology (NR) have a joint project for the designation of doctoral programs that lists those criteria that are necessary for a program to be considered a doctoral training program in psychology (ASPPB and NR, 2005). Graduate programs must apply for this ASPPB and NR designation. These criteria were originally developed from a National Conference on Education and Credentialing in Psychology held in 1977, and although they have been updated, they are included in the licensure laws of most jurisdictions as the basis on which to determine the legitimacy of a psychology program. The curriculum requirements contained in the designation criteria are the most often cited in state and provincial licensure laws. Students should check to see that their program is listed and that they individually have a minimum of 3 years of full-time graduate study with at least 1 year (preferably 2 years) of on-campus residency (NR, 2005). They should have at least 90 semester hours of coursework not including internship hours and should also make certain that in addition to course requirements in their specific area of study (e.g., clinical, counseling, school, I/O, developmental) they also have at least one course in each of the following:

- scientific and professional ethics and standards;
- research design and methodology;
- statistics;
- psychometric theory;
- biological bases of behavior: physiological psychology, comparative psychology, neuropsychology, sensation and perception, and psychopharmacology;
- cognitive–affective bases of behavior: learning, thinking, motivation, and emotion;
- social bases of behavior: social psychology, group processes, organizational and systems theory; and
- individual differences: personality theory, human development, and abnormal psychology.

Students should also have sufficient practicum hours that illustrate both breadth and depth in the practical application of their coursework. Although the number of practicum hours has been increasing over the last several years, a total of 1,000 hours is generally sufficient to obtain an APA- or CPA-accredited internship.

The Internship

It is important to note that even though licensure laws are generic, most licensure laws require 2 years of supervised experience; 1 year may be a predoctoral internship, and 1 year must be postdoctoral in the area of the applicant's program of study (see chap. 6, this volume). In those areas of study in which no internship is required for the degree, both years of supervised experience must be postdoctoral (see chap. 13, this volume).

Most licensure laws require that applicants from an HSP area have a predoctoral internship that is required as a part of their doctoral program, the length of which is no less than 12 months and no more that 24 months. In general, internships are for 1 year full time; however, most laws allow for a 2-year half-time internship as well. Although the number of internship hours required to qualify for licensure varies from 1,500 to 2,000, students are advised to document a full 2,000 hours and to work no less than 50 weeks. Those in half-time internships should document the same hours in no less than 100 weeks. For the protection of the student, APA- or CPA-accredited internships are preferable (APA, 2005b); however, if the internship is not accredited, then it is critical that the internship is a member of the Association of Psychology Postdoctoral and Internship Centers (APPIC, 2005; chap. 6, this volume).

HSP interns must document that there were at least two interns for the entire length of the internship, that they completed 2,000 hours in 50 weeks, that they had at least 500 direct contact hours, and that they were supervised by at least two licensed psychologists for a minimum of 200 hours, 100 hours of which must have been individual supervision, and 100 hours of group or additional individual supervision. Non-HSP interns should document the 2,000 total hours, 500 direct contact hours, and 200 supervision hours, appropriate to the area of study. Both HSP and non-HSP internships should document 100 hours of didactic training as an integral part of the internship program.

Finally, when the internship is completed, every intern must receive a form signed by the director of training (DOT) certifying all of the previously mentioned requirements. ASPPB (2005b) has a very complete and specific form for this purpose that is used for students to bank their internship in preparation for obtaining the Certificate of Professional Qualification in Psychology. It can be downloaded from their Web site at http://www.asppb.org/mobility/pdf/cbapp.pdf (see chap. 9; Appendix C, this volume).

The Postdoctoral Supervision Year

As mentioned in the internship section, even though licensure laws are generic, most licensure laws require 2 years of supervised experience: 1 year may be a predoctoral internship, and 1 year must be postdoctoral in the applicant's program of study. As a reminder, in those areas of study in which no internship is required for the degree, both years of supervised experience must be postdoctoral.

The postdoctoral year of supervision is the most variant as to specific requirements of individual jurisdictional laws, and often the most problematic, for students determining what to do to be sure that they meet the licensure requirements in most, if not all jurisdictions. Even though almost all jurisdictions have changed their laws to reflect the APA and ASPPB Model Acts standard for HSP applicants to 1 year of internship and 1 year of postdoctoral supervision, there remain a handful of jurisdictions that require either 0 (Alabama and Washington, and Newfoundland, Labrador, Quebec, and Saskatchewan in Canada) or 2 years (Delaware, District of Columbia, and Michigan). Therefore, applicants who want to guarantee that they meet the postdoctoral year licensure requirement in all jurisdictions must complete a 2-year postdoctoral supervision experience.

Students who complete a formal postdoctoral year in a position that is either APA accredited or APPIC listed should have no problem in acceptance for licensure. These students will receive the required direct service hours, a minimum of 2 hours per week of individual supervision, and it will be documented and signed by the DOT. The problem is that there are few of these accredited formal postdoctoral positions as compared with the number of students who must complete the postdoctoral year. The vast majority of students will complete their postdoctoral supervision year in an agency, public or private, and will need to document all of their supervision and direct service hours themselves. Students are advised to be absolutely certain that they receive a minimum of 90 minutes, preferably 2 hours, of individual supervision per week. Especially in this circumstance, it is critical that the student's primary supervisor sign documentation indicating the number of hours spent in each activity during the postdoctoral year (see chap. 7, this volume).

Conclusion

More often than any of us who have been the director of training of an academic or internship program would like to admit, we have failed to keep up with the licensure requirements of any jurisdiction other than our own, and at times perhaps not even that. This failure has on occasion left our students vulnerable to denial of licensure when they applied to another state or province. Although it is a practical impossibility to remain current on all licensure requirements of all jurisdictions, it is imperative that we become aware of and provide each and every student with training that meets at least the high standard of licensure requirements across most jurisdictions. To do less is to leave students with a limited professional career and resentment toward the very mentors in whose hands they placed their professional futures.

References

American Psychological Association. (2005a). *Accredited doctoral programs in professional psychology.* Retrieved January 18, 2006, from http://www.apa.org/ed/accreditation/doctoral.html

American Psychological Association. (2005b). *Accredited internship and postdoctoral programs for training in psychology.* Retrieved January 18, 2006, from http://www.apa.org/ed/accreditation/intern.html

American Psychological Association. (2005c). *Guidelines and principles for accreditation of programs in professional psychology.* Retrieved January 18, 2006, from http://www.apa.org/ed/G&p052.pdf

Association of Psychology Postdoctoral and Internship Centers. (2005). *Search the directory online: Internships.* Retrieved January 18, 2006, from http://appic.org/directory/search_dol_internships.asp

Association of State and Provincial Psychology Boards. (2005a). *EPPP exam information. Frequently asked questions: Scores.* Retrieved January 18, 2006, from http://www.asppb.org/epppExam/faq/score.aspx

Association of State and Provincial Psychology Boards. (2005b). *Form 104: Director of predoctoral internship or postdoctoral residency verification form.* Retrieved January 18, 2006, from http://www.asppb.org/mobility/pdf/cpq104.pdf

Association of State and Provincial Psychology Boards. (2005c). *Welcome to the handbook of licensing and certification requirements for psychologists in the United States and Canada.* Retrieved January 18, 2006, from http://www.asppb.org/handbook/handbook.aspx

Association of State and Provincial Psychology Boards and the National Register of Health Service Providers in Psychology. (2005). *Guidelines for defining a doctoral degree in psychology.* Retrieved January 19, 2006, from http://www.nationalregister.org/doctoraldegrees.html

Canadian Psychological Association. (2005). *CPA accredited programs.* Retrieved January 19, 2006, from http://www.cpa.ca/cpasite/ShowPage.asp?id=10042&fr=

Hargrove, D. S. (2003, February). *APA accreditation.* Paper presented at the meeting of the Association of State and Provincial Psychology Boards, San Antonio, TX.

Hess, H. F. (1977). Entry requirements for professional practice of psychology. *American Psychologist, 32,* 365–368.

Jonason, K., DeMers, S., Vaughn, T. J., & Reaves, R. (2003). Professional mobility for psychologists is rapidly becoming a reality. *Professional Psychology: Research and Practice, 34,* 468–473.

Meyer, M. E., & Altmaier, E. M. (1985). Introduction. In E. M. Altmaier & M. E. Meyer (Eds.), *Applied specialties in psychology* (pp. 1–15). New York: Random House.

National Register of Health Service Providers in Psychology. (2005). *ASPPB/National Register Designation Project: Designated doctoral programs in psychology.* Retrieved January 19, 2006, from http://www.nationalregister.org/designate.htm

Vaughn, T. J. (1993). Mobility for North American psychologists. *Register Report, 19*(3), 5–6.

Vaughn, T. J. (1999). California psychologists receive special consideration. *California Psychologist, 32*(1), 24–25.

Waters, M. (2000). California takes first step to meet national accreditation standards. *Monitor on Psychology, 31,* 11.

Wiens, A. N. (1983). Toward a conceptualization of competency assurance. *Professional Practice of Psychology, 4,* 1–15.

Wiens, A. N., & Dorken, H. (1986). Establishing and enforcing standards to assure professional competency. In H. Dorken & Associates (Eds.), *Professional psychology in transition* (pp. 174–199). San Francisco: Jossey-Bass.

Randolph P. Reaves

The History of Licensure of Psychologists in the United States and Canada

2

This chapter is devoted to reviewing more than a half century of work to pass licensure laws for psychologists in the jurisdictions of the United States and Canada. It explains the need for licensure and some of the compromises such as "substantial equivalency" that were made to pass these laws. It also explains the differences between licensure laws and certification laws, and addresses some of the appellate court decisions that have had an impact on the way in which the profession is regulated.

The history of licensure efforts of psychologists is now at least 60 years old. The first licensure law for the profession was passed in Connecticut in 1945. Ontario was the first Canadian province to pass a licensing law for psychologists and did so in 1960.

Now, 50 states, 3 U.S. territories, the District of Columbia, 10 Canadian provinces, and the Northwest Territories have some form of regulatory law for psychologists, and in some jurisdictions, for psychological assistants, associates, or examiners, as well. It is unlikely that any other licensure law will pass in the two countries because the populations of the remaining territories are so small. However, the history of the licensure effort is more than just a list of jurisdictions and dates of legislative enactments. It includes retracing the modern evolution of the practice of a profession and the ways in which the field's practitioners have been identified. It also chronicles the movement of a profession from an academic exercise to the application of scientific principles to every day life.

In taking this trip through history, psychologists are compelled to study the growth and evolution of the Association of State and Provincial Psychology Boards (ASPPB). This organization represents almost all the psychology regulatory boards in the United States and Canada, creates the Examination for Professional Practice in Psychology (EPPP), houses the ASPPB Disciplinary Data System, and presents the viewpoint of licensure boards within the world of professional psychology.

The Need for Licensure or Certification

In today's regulatory circles, virtually everyone agrees that the purpose of a regulatory law is to protect the public from incompetent or unscrupulous practitioners. Historically there were other reasons, including the need for legal recognition of a body of knowledge and the laws' protection of the title used by those possessing that knowledge.

In 1977, Harrie Hess, then a member of the Nevada Board of Examiners in Psychology and later the president of ASPPB, wrote that licensure is a legal process intended to protect the public from harm (Hess, 1977) by achieving three primary objectives:

- setting minimal standards of practitioner competence for entering the profession so that consumers are confident that practitioners have undergone adequate training and experience,
- establishing minimal professional standards for practice that all licensed practitioners meet and means of disciplining practitioners who violate these standards and regulations, and
- defining the profession's scope and members so that unlicensed practice or title use is prevented by persons lacking requisite knowledge or skill. (Meyer & Altmaier, 1985; Wiens, 1983; Wiens & Dorken, 1986)

The impetus for the licensure effort was World War II, when applications of the body of psychological knowledge to everyday activities increased dramatically. This is not to say that the science of psychology had not been applied previously to the activities of individuals or organizations (J. Hall, personal communication, February 6, 2006). Psychological testing of children had begun in the early years of the 20th century. Psychological science was applied to advertising before World

War I, and personnel selection tests were used during that conflict. However, World War II vastly increased the opportunity for the clinical application of psychological skills. The U.S. Veterans Administration (VA) became a large employer of psychologists and was the originator of dozens of internship programs. In fact, Hall noted that the VA, through funding for research and internship training, and the National Institute for Mental Health (NIMH), through research grants and fellowships, brought about the training of more doctors in clinical psychology than in any other era of psychology (American Psychological Association [APA], 1947; Cummings & VandenBos, 1983). The VA created the job title "clinical psychologist." Private practices eventually resulted. Psychologists reasoned that if practitioners were going to offer these services to the general public, then the public must be protected through the police power of the states and provinces. Led by Karl F. Heiser, proponents of a licensing law were first successful in the state of Connecticut. The year was 1945.

NONSTATUTORY BOARDS

The passage of licensing and certification laws did not come easily in most jurisdictions. In many jurisdictions, psychologists' efforts were opposed by psychiatry and organized medicine. More problematic was opposition from within university psychology programs. Many academicians argued that licensing laws would affect academic curricula and restrict academic freedom. While struggling with the passage of a licensure law, many psychological associations sponsored voluntary, nonstatutory boards.

Training at the doctoral level has been the recognized training standard since the Boulder Conference held in 1949 (Raimy, 1950). In some jurisdictions, there was insufficient political support for the doctoral level requirement, and in the latter part of the 1960s and early 1970s, statutes passed that allowed individuals possessing master's degrees and a certain number of years of supervised experience to qualify for licensure or certification at the independent practice level.

GRANDPARENT CLAUSES

Most of the licensure laws passed in the United States and Canada had to address the fact that not all practitioners at the time legislation passed could meet the educational requirements set out in the new law even though those individuals were functioning as psychologists. Practitioners using the title *psychologist* at the time a new law passed had a property right in the use of that title and filed lawsuits to prove that point (*Bloom v. Texas,* 1973; *Hereford v. Farrar,* 1971).

Most "grandfather" clauses identified a window of time during which master's level psychologists could apply and become licensed after which the doctoral level became the standard that all candidates had to meet (*Berger v. Board of Psychologist Examiners*, 1973; *McPhail v. Montana*, 1982).

SUBSTANTIAL EQUIVALENCY

In many jurisdictions, due again to the necessity for political compromise, licensure was available not only to candidates with degrees from programs in psychology but also to those whose education was "substantially equivalent" or obtained in "closely allied fields." Disputes between candidates and state boards of examiners were routine and spawned dozens of lawsuits. Some courts ruled in favor of the boards (*Carroll v. State*, 1978; *Ditullio v. State*, 1978) and others ordered applicants licensed or admitted to the licensing exam (*Board of Psychological Examiners v. Coxe*, 1978; *Cohen v. State*, 1978).

In 1976, former ASPPB President Morton Berger of New York coined the oft-repeated phrase "substantially equivalent is a euphemism for 'not psychology'" (Wellner, 1977, p. 4). In 1977, most of the major organizations within the field considered creating the National Commission on Education and Credentialing in Psychology. The effort to create the commission failed, but the criteria for recognition of a doctoral degree in psychology were identified and substantially agreed on.

Those criteria or guidelines, which have been amended slightly over the years, now form the basis for listing as a designated doctoral program in the joint project known as the ASPPB/National Register Doctoral Program Meeting Designation Criteria. Many regulatory boards have incorporated these criteria into their rules that define acceptable education criteria.

In 1977, Missouri became the last state to pass a licensing law. In Canada, Prince Edward Island, in 1990, became the last province to pass a regulatory law. Regulation of psychologists in the Northwest Territories began in the early 1980s. Puerto Rico was the first U.S. territory to pass a law (1983), Guam was the second in 1989, and the Virgin Islands followed in 1994.

Licensure Versus Certification

The two principal methods legislatures use to regulate a profession are through the passage of either licensure or certification laws. The differences were described by Schomberg (1982) as follows:

Licensing is "the process by which an agency of government grants permission to an individual to engage in a given occupation upon finding that the applicant has attained the minimal degree of competency necessary to ensure that the public health, safety and welfare will be reasonably well protected." Since the law establishing a licensed occupation usually sets forth the "scope of practice" covered by the act, licensing laws are often referred to as "practice acts."

Certification is the process by which a governmental or non-governmental agency or association grants authority to use a specified title to an individual who has met predetermined qualifications. (p. 16)

Political compromise is the most likely reason that certification or "title" laws passed in many jurisdictions. Some notable examples of jurisdictions that initially passed certification laws include Arizona, Florida, Maryland, Mississippi, New York, and Rhode Island. A number of jurisdictions have passed amendments to their statutes and moved from title law jurisdictions to those with practice acts.

IDENTIFYING THOSE RESPONSIBLE FOR REGULATION

In the United States, most licensing laws created boards that originally comprised only psychologists. Often these laws required that one or more board members be employed as professors in psychology programs. Boards created in the United States were typically autonomous and distinctly separated from the psychological associations whose members lobbied for the passage of the statute. In both countries, public or consumer members have been added to the majority of boards.

Board responsibilities have certainly changed over the years. Board members are no longer limited to reviewing transcripts, drafting or grading exams, and participating in an occasional disciplinary hearing. In fact, in some jurisdictions, disciplinary matters now occupy the majority of a board member's time, whereas assessing qualifications is often handled by staff members. Widespread utilization of the Examination for Professional Practice in Psychology (EPPP) has sharply reduced the amount of time board members devote to the actual examination of candidates, except in those jurisdictions in which passage of an oral or additional written exams are required. Board members now are expected to oversee continuing education, promulgate standards of practice and conduct, and, when necessary, monitor practices to ensure continuing competence.

THE ADVENT OF SUNSET LEGISLATION

In 1976, Colorado became the first state in the United States to pass what is commonly known as a sunset law. This is a statute that provides a termination date for state agencies. Agencies can avoid termination if they prove the need for continuation during the sunset audit process.

Often the sunset process became an arena in which those who were unable to qualify for licensure as psychologists could vent their frustrations before legislative committees. In two U.S. jurisdictions, these legislative battles resulted in the termination of the psychology regulatory boards. Those states are Florida (1979) and South Dakota (1980). Both licensing laws were later reenacted, the former in 1981 and the latter in 1982.

Because sunset laws exist in approximately 40 U.S. jurisdictions, every year a substantial number of psychology boards must justify their continued existence. In some jurisdictions the sunset process has been a blessing in disguise. A number of jurisdictions have used the process to strengthen and modernize their practice acts.

Wand (1993) noted that the Canadian boards have not faced the threat of deregulation under such sunset laws nor have the profession's practices been scrutinized by an agency such as the Federal Trade Commission, as is the case in the United States. However, there has been governmental review of the professions, such as the Health Professions Legislation Review in 1989 and the Professional Organizations Committee Under the Ministry of the Attorney General in 1980.

GENERIC VERSUS SPECIALTY LICENSING

In the early years, all psychology licensing laws were generic-type statutes, meaning that licenses were issued as psychologist licenses, not in clinical, counseling, school, or some other specialty area of psychology. Over time, proponents of specialty licensing convinced some legislatures to allow boards to issue licenses in recognized specialties. According to Hall (personal communication, February 6, 2006), Virginia was the first to specialize when in 1966 its 1965 law was amended to add a specialty license in clinical psychology. South Carolina is another example. There, the board is legally mandated to determine each applicant's area or areas of specialization. Choices include clinical, counseling, industrial/organizational, community, school, social, and experimental psychology. Several jurisdictions, including Connecticut, Florida, Ohio, Virginia, and Wisconsin, have statutory authority to license school psychologists at the master's level. By and large, however, in the United States most of the work done in the public schools by "school psychologists" is done by individuals certified by state boards of education.

Judy E. Hall, a former ASPPB president, documented the efforts of a number of U.S. jurisdictions to move from generic practice acts to acts that restrict licensure to individuals who provide direct services to individuals, such as clinical psychologists (e.g., Illinois). She noted in several unpublished articles on the history of specialization in professional psychology:

> In nine states currently, after licensure as a psychologist there is a second title tied to eligibility for third party reimbursement, namely health care/service provider/psychologist (Indiana, Iowa, Kentucky, Missouri, Massachusetts, North Carolina, Oklahoma, Tennessee, Texas), typically for graduates of programs in clinical, counseling, school psychology, or other similar areas (e.g., health, clinical neuropsychology, etc.) and/or those who have met the requirements for credentialing by the National Register of Health Service Providers in Psychology. (For more information, see chap. 11, this volume). Other states are currently considering adopting the health service provider in psychology model. In a few other states (e.g., Virginia, South Carolina), two or more specialty titles are regulated. (personal communication, February 6, 2006)

ASSOCIATION OF STATE AND PROVINCIAL PSYCHOLOGY BOARDS'S ROLE IN LICENSING AND CERTIFICATION

The ASPPB originated in New York City in August 1961. It came into being because of the sponsorship of the American Psychological Association's Board of Professional Affairs Committee on State Examination Procedures (Carlson, 1978). There were 29 charter members, some of which were voluntary, nonstatutory licensing boards. The Annual Meeting of Delegates has continued every year since 1961. From the beginning, the Association was comprised of both Canadian and U.S. boards. C. Roger Myers of Ontario, Canada, was the sixth president of the organization.

One major purpose for the organization of the Association was the creation of a uniform examination for candidates for licensure. A uniform exam was considered essential to the concept of mobility for psychologists.

ASPPB now supports more than a dozen committees and task forces on regulatory issues and internal operations. Liaisons from ASPPB present the perspective of the licensure boards to APA boards such as the Board of Educational Affairs and the Board of Professional Affairs. The Association also sends liaisons to other organizations within the field such as the American Board of Professional Psychology and the Canadian Psychological Association.

ASPPB, in the latter part of the 1990s, developed what has become a very comprehensive Web site, http://www.asppb.org. The Web site is easily accessible and includes information such as the *Handbook of*

Licensing and Certification Requirements for Psychologists in the United States and Canada (http://www.asppb.org/handbook/handbook.aspx; see chap. 3).

In 1983, the organization created the ASPPB Disciplinary Data System. The member boards report all disciplinary sanctions greater than reprimands to ASPPB. The Central Office compiles the data and disseminates it to the member boards and ethics committees of several U.S. and Canadian psychological organizations. It is the only comprehensive disciplinary data bank for psychologists in the world. In 1996, the Association completed the computerization of the data bank. It should also be noted that the United States government, through the passage of the Health Insurance Portability and Accountability Act, created a data bank to which adverse actions taken by psychology licensing boards are now reported.

In 1988, the Association made a tremendous leap in its leadership efforts when President Diane Hill and Executive Officer Paul Reaves were the invited guests of the European Federation of Professional Psychologists Association. This meeting and those that followed eventually led to the First International Congress on the Licensure, Certification, and Credentialing of Psychologists in 1995 and established ASPPB as the worldwide leader in the regulation of the profession. Just as its member boards find that the responsibilities of their members have changed over the years, the same is true of ASPPB. Its responsibility to recommend and promote professional standards has grown enormously. In 1991, under the capable leadership of Norma P. Simon, the ASPPB delegates adopted the *ASPPB Code of Conduct*. A year later, the ASPPB Model Licensure Act was adopted, and even later, a set of model regulations. These documents have served as models for changes in statutory language and rules and regulations. A task force is currently reviewing these documents to address professional advancements such as prescription privileges and telehealth.

THE EXAMINATION PROGRAM

A principle part of ASPPB operations involves the administration of the EPPP to candidates throughout the United States and Canada. As Terris (1973) noted,

> It was intended that the test should establish, nationwide, a minimum standard for certification or licensure and that this common national assessment would provide a basis for reciprocity and/or endorsement of licenses from state to state. (p. 386)

The exam is owned by ASPPB. A 10-member Examination Committee comprising recognized subject matter experts is primarily responsible for each form of the EPPP (see chap. 4, this volume).

Conclusion

The history of licensure of psychologists in the United States and Canada is almost complete, but as the foregoing pages have demonstrated, it is more than just a list of states and dates of legislative enactments. The effort to obtain licensure for the profession had been far more than that, and it has involved thousands of dedicated psychologists, lawyers, and administrators who tirelessly endeavor to improve the process.

References

American Psychological Association. (1947). Recommended graduate training program in clinical psychology. *American Psychologist, 2*, 539–558.

Berger v. Board of Psychologist Examiners for Dist. of Columbia, 313 A.2d 602 (D.C. App. 1973).

Bloom v. Texas State Board of Examiners of Psychologists, 492 S.W.2d 460 (Texas 1973).

Board of Psychological Examiners v. Coxe, 355 So.2d 669 (Miss. 1978).

Carlson, H. S. (1978). The AASPB story: The beginnings and first 16 years of the American Association of State Psychology Boards, 1961–1977. *American Psychologist, 33*, 486–495.

Carroll v. State Board of Examiners of Psychology, 355 So.2d 495 (Fla. App. 1978).

Cohen v. State Board of Psychological Examiners, 588 P.2d 313 (Ariz. App. 1978).

Cummings, N. A., & VandenBos, G. R. (1983). Relations with other professions. In C. E. Walker (Ed.), *Handbook of clinical psychology* (pp. 1301–1327). New York: Dorsey.

Ditullio v. State Board of Examiners of Psychologists, 387 A.2d 757 (Me. 1978).

Hall, J. E. (1995, April). *The emergence of specialties in professional psychology.* Paper presented at the First International Congress on

Licensure, Certification, and Credentialing of Psychologists, New Orleans, LA.

Hereford v. Farrar, 469 S.W.2d 16 (Texas 1971).

Hess, H. F. (1977). Entry requirements for professional practice of psychology. *American Psychologist, 32,* 365–368.

McPhail v. Montana Board of Psychology, 640 P.2d 906 (Montana 1982).

Meyer, M. E., & Altmaier, E. M. (1985). Introduction. In E. M. Altmaier & M. E. Meyer (Eds.), *Applied specialties in psychology* (pp. 1–15). New York: Random House.

Raimy, V. C. (Ed.). (1950). *Training in clinical psychology.* Englewood Cliffs, NJ: Prentice-Hall.

Schomberg, B. (1982). *Occupational licensing: A public perspective.* Princeton, NJ: Educational Testing Service.

Terris, L. D. (1973). The national licensing examination. *Professional Psychology, 4,* 386–391.

Wand, B. (1993). The nature of regulation and entrance criteria. In K. Dobson & D. Dobson (Eds.), *Professional psychology in Canada* (pp. 149–165). Seattle, WA: Hogrefe & Huber.

Wellner, A. M. (Ed.). (1977). Education and credentialing in psychology: II. Report of a meeting, June 4–5, 1977, Washington, DC. *Clinical Psychologist, 31,* 4–10.

Wiens, A. N. (1983). Toward a conceptualization of competency assurance. *Professional Practice of Psychology, 4*(2), 1–15.

Wiens, A. N., & Dorken, H. (1986). Establishing and enforcing standards to assure professional competency. In H. Dorken & Associates (Eds.), *Professional psychology in transition* (pp. 174–199). San Francisco: Jossey-Bass.

Barbara A. Van Horne

Resources Available From the Association of State and Provincial Psychology Boards

3

This chapter covers the extensive resources available from the Association of State and Provincial Psychology Boards (ASPPB), including a model act and rules; licensing exam information; a "summary of licensure requirements"; online guidelines for students, faculty, regulators, and consumers of psychological services; as well as information on the ASPPB and the National Register of Health Service Providers in Psychology (NR) Designation Project.

ASPPB is the alliance of state, provincial, and territorial agencies responsible for the licensure and certification of psychologists throughout the United States and Canada. ASPPB was formed in 1961 to serve psychology boards in the two countries. The impetus for its founding was to create and maintain a standardized written Examination for Professional Practice in Psychology (EPPP) and to create mobility for licensees. ASPPB's mission is to assist its member boards in protecting the public.

In addition to creating the EPPP, ASPPB coordinates cooperative efforts of boards, facilitates communication among boards, maintains a Disciplinary Data Bank, advocates for the advancement of mobility by encouraging board acceptance of the Certificate of Professional Qualification in Psychology (CPQ; see also chap. 9, this volume) and the ASPPB Agreement of Reciprocity, maintains a Credentials

Bank, and provides the EPPP Score Transfer Service. ASPPB acts as a voice for those responsible for the regulation of the practice of psychology. A primary service to its member boards and others has been the provision of documents created by ASPPB staff and committees. ASPPB also generates a number of publications to aid psychology students in preparing for licensure and maintains an online presence at http://www.asppb.org/. ASPPB provides three major types of resources: printed documents, the ASPPB Web site, and the ASPPB staff.

Since its inception, ASPPB has been committed to serving member boards by providing resources to those involved in the education and training of psychologists, psychology students, trainees, candidates for licensure, licensees, and other professional psychology organizations, as well as the public.

Graduate School

ASPPB has taken a major role in the development, utilization, and integration of credentialing and training models, examinations, and other assessment methodologies to establish criteria for psychology licensure and certification. It is the wise student who considers licensure implications throughout the education and training process, beginning with the selection of a graduate program. In many jurisdictions, candidates for licensure must document graduation from a program that is either accredited by the American Psychological Association (APA) or the Canadian Psychological Association (CPA), or designated by the ASPPB–NR Designation Project. The listing identifies the doctoral programs in psychology that have been reviewed by the ASPPB–NR Designation Committee and meet the designation criteria, *Guidelines for Defining a Doctoral Degree in Psychology* (ASPPB and NR, 2004). Graduates of designated programs typically will meet the educational requirements for licensing if they have paid careful attention to fulfilling the curriculum criteria listed in the guidelines. In addition to communications with university officials, department chairs, and program directors, the ASPPB–NR Designation Project relies on publicly available information from university catalogues, program descriptions, brochures, and other official materials (both published and online) submitted by programs. This information should be considered when considering which graduate program best fits professional goals.

Similarly, the ASPBB–NR Designation Project has developed the *ASPPB–NR Criteria for Defining an ASPPB–National Register Designated Postdoctoral Program in Psychopharmacology* (ASPPB and NR, 2005). This is a useful reference when considering a proficiency in clinical psychopharmacology or, in the future, obtaining prescriptive authority (see chap. 14, this volume).

Evaluation of the program can be assisted by reviewing the ASPPB document, *Psychology Licensing Exam Scores by Doctoral Program*, formerly the *Educational Reporting Service Listing: EPPP Performance by Designated Doctoral Program in Psychology* (ASPPB, 2003a), which compares performance of Designated Doctoral Program graduates on the EPPP since 1988, including the number of candidates from each program and, when that number is three or greater, the mean and standard deviation of those scores. The score comparisons are updated annually. The document lists scores by content area and allows the reader to compare the EPPP scores of graduates from colleges and universities that offer a doctoral degree in psychology.

Entry to the Profession

During graduate school, it is important to begin consideration of long-term professional goals. Even prior to internship, some understanding of the requirements for licensure can save later frustration. *Entry Requirements for the Professional Practice of Psychology* (ASPPB, 2001a) is a booklet created to educate psychology students about general legal requirements for licensure or certification to practice the profession. It explores the purpose of such laws and their implementation in the states and provinces. It includes general instructions on preparing for licensure.

In addition, more thorough information is available. *The Handbook of Licensing and Certification Requirements for Psychologists in the United States and Canada* (ASPPB, 2002a) contains the basic requirements for licensure or certification in 53 U.S. jurisdictions and 10 Canadian provinces. It sets out the educational, examination, and experience requirements of each jurisdiction and is now available exclusively at http://www.asppb.org/. The handbook contains other information including Web site addresses, mailing addresses, and telephone numbers of state and provincial boards as well as citations to the relevant statutes creating such boards.

Horror stories abound of trainees who made assumptions about requirements for the number of hours of supervised experience and discover when applying for licensure that the number of hours of face-to-face supervision are greater than obtained, so they must repeat the hours of supervision. There are myriad examples of those not attending to specific coursework requirements who must take another graduate course to be licensed. Thus, it is essential to be aware of not only the general requirements for licensure but also those of the jurisdiction of initial licensure. For further information about procedures and requirements for licensure and scheduling of examinations, a candidate should always contact the psychology licensing or certification board in the state or province in which licensure or certification is being sought. A roster of licensing board addresses is also available at the ASPPB Web site.

Almost all jurisdictions require passage of the EPPP for licensure that ASPPB created and maintains (Rosen, 2000). ASPPB offers several documents to provide information to facilitate successful completion of the EPPP (see chap. 4, this volume). Students preparing to take the EPPP can learn when they are eligible to take the EPPP in each jurisdiction by reviewing the information in the handbook or contacting the local jurisdiction.

Information for Candidates (ASPPB, 2003b) is a brochure available to all candidates for licensure. ASPPB provides *Information for Candidates* to each licensing board for individuals who register to take the EPPP in their jurisdiction. This booklet provides an explanation of the purposes of the examination and describes the construction, content, and administration of the exam. It includes a content outline for the exam, ASPPB exam policies, information on the Score Transfer Service and ASPPB's Examination Committee, as well as sample EPPP questions. *Information for Candidates* is available as a free download on the ASPPB Web site in both English and French.

Some candidates for licensure purchase EPPP preparation materials. ASPPB publishes *Items From Previous Examinations* (ASPPB, 2003c), which contains 250 retired items from the EPPP and an answer key for those items. It also contains a content outline for the exam and the percentage of exam questions contained in each content area. Also included is a list of some but not necessarily all of the references and texts used by the ASPPB Examination Committee in preparing and reviewing examination items. This is available for purchase from ASPPB. ASPPB also offers two computer-administered practice exams, which can help candidates become comfortable with the computer-based testing environment. A practice exam application is available on the Web site.

The following Exhibit 3.1 shows EPPP items obtained from a set of sample items developed to provide guidelines for EPPP item writers for illustrative purposes only (answers follow the items in brackets).

Other documents developed by ASPPB for those applying to take the EPPP include *Frequently Asked Questions for Candidates,* which is a

EXHIBIT 3.1

Sample EPP Items

A husband brings his wife home from the hospital following her right hemisphere stroke. He repeatedly is puzzled by her lack of reaction to his presence when he enters the bedroom. She responds to him when he opens the window across the room. Her behavior is likely explained by:

1. Prosopagnosia.
2. Neglect syndrome.
3. Disassociation apraxia.
4. Capgrass syndrome.

[correct answer 2]

A client reports a disturbing dream in which he is chased by a tiger at a circus and rescued by a clown. A gestalt therapist would explore the dream material by encouraging the client to:

1. Become each dream figure.
2. Associate freely to dream figures.
3. Interpret the symbols in the dream.
4. Explore the dream figures through art forms.

[correct answer 1]

Note. Sample test items copyright 2003 by Professional Examination Service. Reprinted with permission.

section on the ASPPB Web site regularly updated to address concerns and explain purposes of the EPPP and procedures for applying, and the *Questions and Answers About Computer-Based Administration of the Examination for Professional Practice in Psychology,* which addresses many issues raised when encountering the computerized exam. One of the most frequently asked questions is, "What does my score mean?" Check out the conversion table on the ASPPB Web site. Another frequently asked question is, "How long do I have for the exam?" The answer is 4 hours, 15 minutes. There is an additional 15 minutes for the tutorial that is not counted in the total test time. Another question is, "Where do I take the test?" There are more than 320 Prometric Technology Centers in the United States and Canada. Candidates may access a test site locator tool at http://www.prometric/.com. One question, "When will I get my score?" is responsive to candidates' needs for timely information; ASPPB has now authorized Professional Examination Service (PES) to report scores twice a month. Another question is, "Is there a way to apply for the EPPP online?" The current answer is no, but that service is being developed. Thus, ASPPB not only provides resources but also financially supports procedures to expedite the examination experience for candidates for licensure (R. Lipkins, personal communication, August 1, 2005).

Clinical Practice: From Practica to Retirement

Just as it is essential to be mindful of licensure requirements when selecting a graduate program, it is also prudent to consider the licensing requirements for supervised experience. It is also important to assure that the training is a qualified and quality experience. The ASPPB publication, *The Report of the Task Force on Supervision Guidelines* (Pacht, Leffler, McLaughlin, & Van Horne, 1998), contains information regarding supervision of unlicensed personnel, including doctoral-level licensure candidates, nondoctoral personnel, and uncredentialed personnel. The supervision guidelines are useful for supervisors and supervisees and are available on the Web site. The full task force report, which includes the guidelines, references, and supplemental material, is exclusively available in printed form.

During all supervised experience, including practica, and throughout clinical practice, adherence to ethical practice is essential. In addition to the APA "Ethical Principles of Psychologists and Code of Conduct" (APA, 2002; see also online version at http://www.apa.org/ethics/) and the CPA *Ethical Codes of Conduct* (CPA, 2000; see also online version at http://www.cpa.ca/cpasite/userfiles/Documents/Canadian%20Code%20of%20Ethics%20for%20Psycho.pdf/), the following ASPPB publications can be of assistance in handling the complexities and challenges of adherence to standards of practice.

The *ASPPB Code of Conduct* (ASPPB, 2004) was adopted in 1990 as a set of suggested guidelines that jurisdictions may reference or incorporate to govern the professional conduct of licensees. This publication was revised in 2001 and again in 2004. This code, which is available on the Web site, is an excellent companion to the APA and CPA ethical codes, as it is designed for regulation of the ethical practice of psychologists. Another tool is the *Ethical Dilemmas Facing Psychologists* (Simon et al., 1996), a 40-minute videotape available for purchase, designed to promote discussion of ethical dilemmas. Its five segments cover several ethical issues accompanied by inappropriate and appropriate resolutions by the psychologist involved. *Professional Conduct and Discipline in Psychology* (Bass et al., 1996) is a companion book complementary to the video. *Professional Conduct and Discipline in Psychology* outlines ethical dilemmas, offers strategies for handling them, and details possible consequences of acting in an unethical manner. In addition to historical background on professional licensure and codes of ethics, this text provides information on education and training; licensing, certification, and credentialing; common ethical dilemmas; methods of maintaining ethical practice, such as self-evaluation and peer review; regulation of practice; and liability for inappropriate behavior. The book also introduces issues expected to affect psychology practice in the future. It is published jointly by ASPPB and APA and can be ordered from APA Books at http://www.apa.org/books.

Another document, *Avoiding Liability in Mental Health Practice* (Reaves, 2004), provides descriptions and case law references in more than 35 topics to aid practitioners in recognizing and avoiding pitfalls and dilemmas that lead to liability in mental health practice. Topics include failure to warn, confidentiality, informed consent, and many others in the civil area. This publication is available for purchase and includes material relating to criminal, license-related, and tax liability.

ASPPB developed the Disciplinary Data System (DDS) in 1983 to provide a repository of disciplinary actions as reported by member boards. All psychologists who have been the subject of a public discipline are reported to the DDS. This resource is not only a service to member boards, who check on disciplinary status of candidates for licensure, but also a foundation for analyses of misconduct and continuing education needs of psychologists. This is not available to the public.

Licensure and Mobility

ASPPB encourages and fosters the mutual recognition of standards of credentials to practice psychology among member boards. It is important that graduate students and trainees consider their long-term possibilities regarding where and how they might practice psychology. A psychologist must be licensed in each state or province in which he or she provides services or performs activities that fall within the scope of practice of the psychology licensure or practice act in that jurisdiction; therefore, recognition of requirements beyond the initial license is essential. Because of differences in requirements among jurisdictions, and because requirements for licensure have changed over time, licensure in additional jurisdictions may not always be as simple as a practitioner assumes it will be or thinks it should be. ASPPB maintains four programs to facilitate professional mobility for licensed doctoral-level psychologists.

The ASPPB Credentials Bank allows information pertaining to education, training, and experience to be archived. Students who begin to archive their credentials right after internship, then add the transcript, then the verification of the postdoctoral supervised experience, will establish a full record of preparation for licensure that will be available for initial licensure or at any time in the future (see chap. 9, this volume).

The CPQ is based on the individual psychologist meeting core licensure criteria, including having been licensed for at least 5 years. A CPQ holder is thereby not required to document their exam scores, transcripts, and supervised experience over and over again each time they move to or practice in a new state or province that accepts the CPQ.

In contrast, the ASPPB Agreement of Reciprocity is based on participating states and provinces bringing their licensure requirements into conformity with the standards in the agreement and accepting each others' licensees. A psychologist who holds a license in one participating jurisdiction may obtain a license in another participating jurisdiction without having to provide transcripts or experience documentation.

Through its Score Transfer Service, ASPPB provides individuals the ability to report their EPPP scores to states and provinces in addition to those in which they were initially licensed. The score report is coupled with a disciplinary data check on the transferee. ASPPB provides this service in an effort not only to serve licensees and its member boards but also to protect consumers of psychological services.

Other Helpful Publications

ASPPB is committed to providing information and guidance to member boards, training programs, the media, the public, governmental bodies, and other entities regarding regulatory, professional, and legislative issues through the development of models for the regulation of psychologists as well as guidelines for practice. The following are examples of the documents available. ASPPB has developed documents (*ASPPB Code of Conduct*, ASPPB, 2004; *Model Act for Licensure of Psychologists*, ASPPB, 2001b; *Model Regulations*, ASPPB, 2002b) for use by member boards as a prototype for of licensing laws and rules in the United States and Canada. Many member boards have adopted elements in their regulations.

The *Model Act for Licensure of Psychologists* features a licensure act template, which psychology boards have found useful when drafting their governing laws and regulations. This publication includes language regarding continuing professional educational requirements, interjurisdictional practice, health service providers, and numerous other regulatory issues. The *ASPPB Model Regulations* have been developed to complement the *ASPPB Model Act of Licensure for Psychologists* and supply the detailed sections that jurisdictions might find helpful in developing either new regulations or changes in regulations. Included are sections on prescription privileges and telehealth practice.

In addition, ASPPB committees and task forces have produced guidelines to facilitate regulations as well as to inform candidates and licensees of models for specific aspects of licensing regulations. Of specific relevance to students and trainers are the ASPPB *Supervision Guidelines*. All guidelines listed here may be purchased in bound edition, but they are also available for free on the Web site (Greenberg, Smith, & Muenzen, 1996; Greenberg, Smith, Muenzen, & Jesuitus, 2003; Melynk, Loucks, Nutt, O'Connor, Yarrow, & Pacht, 1999).

Continuing Professional Education Guidelines (Melnyk et al., 2001b) is a publication prepared to assist licensing boards establishing new, or enhancing existing, continuing education requirements, as well as to encourage consistency across jurisdictions. The guidelines include specific recommendations for regulations as well as a review of the history and current status of continuing education.

The *ASPPB Guidelines for Prescriptive Authority* (Melnyk et al., 2001a) was prepared to assist boards in maintaining as much consistency as possible when they write regulations for prescriptive authority. Included are sections on the history and current status of the move toward prescription privileges, legal issues, parameters of prescriptive practice, and approaches for regulating prescriptive privileges, curriculum, examination, and supervised experience. An excellent bibliography and extensive appendixes are included.

The ASPPB Web site offers a number of documents intended for use by consumers of psychological services. Many products were obtained from the California Board of Psychology for use by other member boards.

Professional Relations

ASPPB is committed to communicating and collaborating with other professional psychology and regulatory organizations, especially regarding education, training, and mobility of psychologists. It is often through these dialogues that trends and concerns about licensing regulations can be addressed. ASPPB maintains a liaison relationship with many organizations involved with the education and training of students.

The following are professional organizations with which ASPPB has formal liaison relationships: American Board of Professional Psychology (ABPP), APA (including APA Advisory Committee on Colleague

Assistance), American Psychological Association of Graduate Students (APAGS), Board of Educational Affairs, Board of Professional Affairs, Committee for the Advancement of Professional Practice, Association of Psychology Postdoctoral and Internship Centers, Council of Chairs of Training Councils, Council of Credentialing Organizations in Professional Psychology, CPA, Canadian Register of Health Service Providers in Psychology, Council of Provincial Associations of Psychology, European Federation of Psychologists Associations, National Council of Schools and Programs of Professional Psychology, Psychology Executives Roundtable, Society for Industrial and Organizational Psychology, and the Trilateral Forum. In addition, ASPPB collaborates regularly with other psychology organizations such as the National Register of Health Service Providers in Psychology and the Council for University Directors in Clinical Psychology.

Liaison relationships can include attendance at board meetings, membership meetings, or both. In some cases, there is a corresponding-only relationship. ASPPB funds participation by a liaison from the APAGS to attend an ASPPB Board of Directors meeting and membership meeting. Those dialogues influence ASPPB ability to be responsive to the needs of candidates for licensure.

ASPPB is committed to open communication with other professional organizations, including participation at such meetings as the APA Consolidated Meetings as well as the APA Education Leadership and the APA State Leadership meetings, as vehicles to learn about and speak to trends and issues facing the profession and the regulation of psychologists.

Future Resources of the Association of State and Provincial Psychology Boards

As ASPPB enhances its Web site and use of electronic communications, more information will be available and will be more easily updated. The mission of ASPPB is to assist member boards in protecting the public. To achieve that goal, the association must inform candidates for licensure. The ASPPB is the natural resource for students regarding licensure and certification.

The ASPPB offers many resources to students and candidates for licensure. Not only can ASPPB's documents provide essential information about the EPPP and requirements for licensure, the Web site also provides links to licensing agencies and other relevant psychology organizations. When students of psychology think of ASPPB, they know answers to their questions are only a click away. Practicing good risk management means being aware of licensure expectations while in training. Accessing ASPPB for resources is insurance for the future.

References

American Psychological Association. (2002). Ethical principles of psychologists and code of conduct. *American Psychologist, 47*, 1597–1611.

Association of State and Provincial Psychology Boards. (2001a). *Entry requirements for the professional practice of psychology* [Brochure]. Montgomery, AL: Author.

Association of State and Provincial Psychology Boards. (2001b). *Model act for licensure for psychologists* (3rd ed.). Montgomery, AL: Author.

Association of State and Provincial Psychology Boards. (2002a). *Handbook of licensing and certification requirements for psychologists in the United States and Canada* (11th ed.). Montgomery, AL: Author.

Association of State and Provincial Psychology Boards. (2002b). *Model regulations for licensure for psychologists.* Montgomery, AL: Author.

Association of State and Provincial Psychology Boards. (2003a). *Educational reporting service listing: EPPP performance by designated doctoral program in psychology* (13th ed.). Montgomery, AL: Author.

Association of State and Provincial Psychology Boards. (2003b). *Information for candidates* [Brochure]. Montgomery, AL: Author.

Association of State and Provincial Psychology Boards. (2003c). *Items from previous examinations.* Montgomery, AL: Author.

Association of State and Provincial Psychology Boards. (2004). *ASPPB code of conduct* (3rd ed.). Montgomery, AL: Author.

Association of State and Provincial Psychology Boards and the National Register of Health Services Providers in Psychology Designation Project. (2004). *Guidelines for defining a doctoral degree in psychology.* Retrieved January 6, 2006, from http://www.nationalregister.org/designate.htm

Association of State and Provincial Psychology Boards and the National Register of Health Services Providers in Psychology. (2005). *Criteria for defining an ASPPB/National Register designated postdoctoral program in psychopharmacology.* Retrieved January 6, 2006, from http://www.nationalregister.org/RXPCriteria_Oct3_Final.pdf

Bass, L. J., DeMers, S. T., Ogloff, J. R., Peterson, C., Pettifor, J., Reaves, R. P., et al. (1996). *Professional conduct and discipline in psychology.* Washington, DC: American Psychological Association.

Canadian Psychological Association. (2000). *Canadian code of ethics for psychologists* (3rd ed.). Retrieved March 22, 2006, from http://www.cpa.ca/cpasite/userfiles/Documents/Canadian%20Code%20of%20Ethics%20for%20Psycho.pdf

Greenberg, S., Smith, I. L., & Muenzen, P. M. (1996). *Study of the practice of licensed psychologists in the United States and Canada.* New York: Professional Examination Service.

Greenberg, S., Smith, I. L., Muenzen, P. M., & Jesuitus, L. (2003). *Study of the practice of licensed psychologists in the United States and Canada.* (2nd ed.). New York: Professional Examination Service.

Melnyk, W. T., Allen, M. T., Nutt, R. L., O'Connor, T., Robiner, W., Linder-Crow, J., & Pacht, A. (2001a). *ASPPB guidelines for prescriptive authority.* Montgomery, AL: Association of State and Provincial Psychology Boards.

Melnyk, W. T., Allen, M. T., Nutt, R. L., O'Connor, T., Robiner, W., Linder-Crow, J., & Pacht, A. (2001b). *Continuing professional education guidelines.* Montgomery, AL: Association of State and Provincial Psychology Boards.

Melnyk, W. T., Loucks, S., Nutt, R. L., O'Connor, T., Yarrow, C., & Pacht, A. (1999). *Oral examination guidelines.* Montgomery, AL: Association of State and Provincial Psychology Boards.

Pacht, A., Leffler, B., McLaughlin, R. E., & Van Horne, B. (1998). *Report of the ASPPB task force on supervision guidelines.* Montgomery, AL: Association of State and Provincial Psychology Boards.

Reaves, R. P. (2004). *Avoiding liability in mental health practice.* Montgomery, AL: Association of State and Provincial Psychology Boards.

Rosen, G. A. (2000). *Research digest: The examination for professional practice.* Montgomery, AL: Association of State and Provincial Psychology Boards.

Simon, N. P., DeMers, S. T., Bass, L., Peterson, C., Pettifor, J., Reaves, R. P., et al. (1996). *Ethical dilemmas facing psychologists.* Montgomery, AL: Association of State and Provincial Psychology Boards.

Lynn P. Rehm and Robert H. Lipkins

The Examination for Professional Practice in Psychology

4

The Association of State and Provincial Psychology Boards (ASPPB), originally the American Association of State Psychology Boards, was founded in 1961 with one of its missions to create a national licensure exam. A committee was formed to develop an outline for the exam and to write items to meet the exam outline. In 1965 Form 1 of the Examination for Professional Practice in Psychology (EPPP) was created and administered to 27 candidates in 8 states. From the outset, the EPPP comprised multiple-choice items in examination forms varying from 150 to 200 items, with a new form created every 2 years. The exam standard became 200 items, and through the 1980s and 1990s two forms per year were offered in paper-and-pencil format in April and October. Today the exam is offered to more than 4,000 candidates per year in 62 jurisdictions in Canada, the United States, and its territories.

Currently, the EPPP is made up of 225 items, of which the extra 25 sets of items are being pretested and are not scored. Candidates have 4 hours and 15 minutes to complete the exam. The EPPP is administered at the candidates' preferred time at Prometric sites all over the United States and Canada. Two new forms are rotated into the four operating forms each year that are preequated to a pass point equivalent to an earlier target form. Scores are reported as scaled scores with a range from 200 to 800 and a pass point of 500.

What Does the Exam Test?

Since its inauguration in 1964, every effort has been made to ensure the validity of the EPPP. The meticulous test development process constitutes one major facet of the validation effort, one devoted to the assurance of content validity. The relationship between the test scores and certain candidate characteristics is periodically reviewed. A digest of validation research is available from ASPPB on their Web site at http://www.asppb.org/.

Several studies have been carried out to develop appropriate test specifications for the EPPP. The first was a role delineation study performed in 1982 (Richman, 1982) for the purpose of developing practice-relevant test specifications. This purpose was achieved by two blue-ribbon panels that defined the performance domains, roles, and knowledge required for generic, entry-level practice in psychology. The second study, a job analysis performed in 1983 by Rosenfeld, Shimberg, and Thornton, resulted in the description of the dimensions of psychological practice among licensed practitioners representing clinical, counseling, industrial/organizational (I/O), and school psychologists.

The present test structure was the result of a third project by Greenberg, Smith, and Muenzen (1996). On the basis of the findings of the two previous studies, this project developed a content outline to guide the construction of each examination. This project was accomplished by a 25-member panel representing the major practice areas in psychology. Panel members participated in a three-stage process in the course of which the roles, responsibilities, and major dimensions of practice were defined. Knowledge statements derived from the previous role delineation and practice analysis were rated for importance, criticality, and appropriateness for entry-level practice in a large-scale survey of licensed psychologists in the United States and Canada. This validation survey represented the judgments of more than 3,900 psychologists. Surviving knowledge statements were linked to dimensions of practice. A subcommittee of eight panel members then met to review the project and to evaluate the domains and responsibilities to arrive at final weightings and to produce the final product of the project. The practice analysis described earlier also yielded an outline of various roles and responsibilities undertaken by practicing psychologists.

An update to the practice analysis was completed in June 2003 by Greenberg and DeJesuitus (2003). An advisory committee determined eight special areas of interest in psychology that should be represented in an update study. An eight-member task force reviewed and revised the delineation of roles and responsibilities as well as content areas and knowledge statements. Empirical evidence was gathered through critical incident interviews, focus panels, and a validation survey sent to more than 1,000 licensed psychologists in the United States and Canada. Respondents were requested to rate the components of the test specifications on importance, frequency, criticality, and point of acquisition. As a result of the data-collection process, the ASPPB approved the use of the content areas and knowledge statements as the primary organizing structure, and revised percentage weights for two of the eight content areas of the exam.

Table 4.1 shows the overall content outline that provides the structure for the exam. More detailed knowledge statements provide guidance to candidates as to what kinds of specific content areas are tested. This information can be found on the ASPPB Web site. A second dimension of exam content consists of psychologist role categories and responsibility statements under each role. The role statements are shown in Table 4.2. More specific responsibilities can be found at the ASPPB Web site. The roles and responsibilities are not used in structuring the exam, but they may be guidelines for students and for item writers as to the scope of the EPPP. The items submitted by item writers are linked to the content outline by a system of rubric codes and then double checked by review teams. The appropriate classification of items allows for the assembly of a test that mirrors the description of practice that emerges from the most recent practice analysis study previously described.

Where Do the Items Come From?

Test items that appear on the EPPP go through a lengthy process of review and testing before they become scoreable items. The initial step in this process occurs at item development workshops. These workshops are periodically organized to generate new items for the exam. The

TABLE 4.1

Content Outline of the Examination for Professional Practice in Psychology

Rubric	Content area	Percentage of the exam[a]
01	Biological bases of behavior: knowledge of (a) biological and neural bases of behavior, (b) psychopharmacology, and (c) methodologies supporting this body of knowledge.	11
02	Cognitive–affective bases of behavior: knowledge of (a) cognition and its neural bases; (b) theories and empirical bases of learning, memory, motivation, affect, emotion, and executive function; and (c) factors that influence cognitive performance or emotional experience and their interaction.	13
03	Social and multicultural bases of behavior: knowledge of (a) intrapersonal, interpersonal, intragroup, and intergroup processes and dynamics; (b) theories of personality; and (c) issues in diversity.	12
04	Growth and lifespan development: knowledge of (a) age-appropriate development across the life span, (b) atypical patterns of development, and (c) the protective and risk factors that influence developmental outcomes for individuals.	13
05	Assessment and diagnosis: knowledge of (a) psychometrics; (b) assessment models and instruments; (c) assessment methods for initial status of and change by individuals, couples, families, groups, and organizations or systems; and (d) diagnostic classification systems and their limitations.	14
06	Treatment, intervention, and prevention: knowledge of (a) individual, couple, family, group, organizational, or community interventions for specific concerns or disorders in diverse populations; (b) intervention and prevention theories; (c) best practices; and (d) consultation models and processes.	15
07	Research methods and statistics: knowledge of (a) research design, methodology, and program evaluation; (b) instrument selection and validation; and (c) statistical models, assumptions, and procedures.	7
08	Ethical, legal, and professional issues: knowledge of (a) codes of ethics, (b) professional standards for practice, (c) legal mandates and restrictions, (d) guidelines for ethical decision making, and (e) professional training and supervision.	15

[a]As approved by the Association of State and Provincial Psychology Boards Board of Directors, June 21, 2003.

workshops are organized by the Professional Examination Service (PES), and the ASPPB provides subject matter experts. Typically these workshops are organized around a particular theme or content area within psychology, (e.g., ethics, neuropsychology, etc.). Authors write items in advance of the workshop and check the validity of each other's

TABLE 4.2

Psychologist Roles and Responsibilities

Rubric	Roles	Approximate percentage
01	Psychological services: Design or provide psychological services, or supervise or manage their delivery, to individuals, couples, families, groups, organizations, or systems in a manner consistent with current professional and ethical standards and guidelines, and jurisdictional and national laws and regulations.	74
02	Consultation, outreach, and policy making: Prepare, present, coordinate, and evaluate educational and training programs for public or organizational audiences; disseminate information or provide expertise to a variety of constituents; and participate in the process of policy making, advocacy, and standard setting in a manner consistent with current professional and ethical standards and guidelines, and jurisdictional and national laws and regulations.	9
03	Academic preparation and professional development: Develop, implement, administer, and evaluate educational programs for psychologists including teaching, supervision, and curriculum development in a manner consistent with current professional and ethical standards and guidelines, and jurisdictional and national laws and regulations; engage in continuing education and self-development.	10
04	Research, evaluation, and scholarship: Develop, participate, or both, in any activity to expand or refine knowledge or to improve programs and services in a manner consistent with current professional and ethical standards and guidelines, and jurisdictional and national laws and regulations.	7

items at the workshop. Items may also be solicited individually from psychologists who have expertise in a specific area.

Training in writing multiple-choice items is provided by PES psychometricians. Writers are trained to write items that conform to commonly accepted standards of item writing (Haladyna, 1999; Haladyna, Downing, & Rodriquez, 2002).

The validation process consists of rating each item on 5 rating scales. The first 3 scales relate to level of mastery, importance, and the contribution to public protection made by the knowledge tested in the item. The second set of scales refers to the appropriateness of item content for all candidate groups and the presence of content that might be offensive or reinforce common stereotypes. Additional questions address the accuracy of the keyed answer and whether the content of the item is equally appropriate for Canadian and U.S. psychologists.

Items may be edited or revised at the workshops to improve their accuracy, readability, or a variety of other factors. Items must be grammatically correct and not include any inadvertent cues that would tip off a testwise candidate that a particular alternative might be a correct answer or incorrect answer. Such clues may permit a candidate with only partial knowledge of the topic to get the question correct.

Each item must have a reference that supports the accuracy of the correct answer. Each item is classified according to cognitive level. The cognitive level of the item is based on a modified version of Bloom's Taxonomy of Educational Objectives (Bloom, Englehart, Furst, Hill, & Krathwohl, 1956). Items are classified as being at the knowledge level (recall or recognition) or at higher levels of complexity (application, analysis or problem-solving). Last, each item is linked to the test specification document by a series of rubric codes.

At the conclusion of the item development workshop, all accepted items are entered into a computerized item banking system at PES. Items undergo additional psychometric review by PES psychometric and editorial staff.

Before items can be used as active items on an exam, they must be pretested. Groups of 25 items are assembled as pretest blocks and exposed along with live items. Pretest items are not scored as part of an examination, but performance data is gathered on them. Pretest items undergo further review by members of the ASPPB examination committee before they appear on an examination. After pretest items have been exposed to a predetermined number of test takers, item performance statistics are computed. These analyses include generation of classical item statistics as well as item parameters following models of Item Response Theory. Items are reviewed by PES psychometricians and examination committee members. Pretested items may then be used on an examination form. After pretesting, some items are revised to improve their quality and are pretested again.

Draft examinations are assembled by PES psychometricians. The draft examinations consist of a mix of previously used items and recently pretested and calibrated items. The draft examinations are reviewed on at least two separate occasions by the full examination committee. The committee may remove items from the draft exam and replace them with other items from the calibrated portion of the item bank. Once examinations are finalized, they are mounted on Prometric's computer testing system where they will be assigned to candidates in the United States and Canada. Four different forms of the EPPP are available at any one time. Every 6 months, the oldest form is retired and a new form is exposed.

How Is Each Exam Form Reviewed Prior to Administration?

The Examination Committee is made up of 10 psychologists from the United States and Canada with expertise in the various domains of professional psychology. They are responsible for the specific item content of the exam. Formerly administered twice a year (in April and October) in paper-and-pencil format, the EPPP is available continuously at Prometric computerized testing centers. The exam committee meets twice a year and reviews the tests item by item for validity of content (keyed answer correct and distracters incorrect), grammar and readability, currency, level of difficulty (too easy or too specialized for the novice psychologist), and criticality to protection of the public. In making these judgments, the committee is aided by test statistics for each item for each previous use, a specific reference for the authority for the item, and item classification data. The examination committee has access to a basic library of authoritative references and PsychLit online to check facts and references.

The resulting examinations consist of 200 multiple-choice items (four choices per item) in eight groups matching the published examination specifications. Twenty-five unscored pretest items are also included to bring the total number of items to 225. As a high-stakes exam, many candidates find it a stressful experience.

Who Constructs and Administers the Exam?

The PES is the test construction contractor for the ASPPB. PES originated in 1941 as the testing department of the American Public Health Association (APHA). As an APHA testing department, PES focused on providing examinations for health professionals employed by state and local civil service agencies. In 1971, PES became an independent not-for-profit corporation and began to expand its client base to include organizations that license and certify health and allied health professionals on a national basis. PES's clients span a wide range of professions, industries, and skill levels including business, industrial, and government sectors. PES maintains the EPPP item bank; assists ASPPB in the development of examination forms; conducts practice analysis studies and other validity-related research; administers the application process to take the examination; and provides scoring, scaling, and reporting of EPPP test scores to jurisdictions and candidates.

The EPPP is currently administered by the Thomson Prometric Corporation. Prometric began in 1990 when the company, then known as Drake, developed a computerized examination for information technology accreditation. Drake was purchased by Sylvan Learning Systems in 1997, and as Prometric began to further expand its presence in the academic and professional test development and test delivery business. During this era, Prometric began building a global testing network to support a growing demand from large testing organizations. In March 2000 Prometric was acquired by The Thomson Corporation. Today, Prometric is the exclusive testing partner for several large and prestigious organizations developing tests in education, industry, and health fields. Prometric maintains several networks to conduct computerized testing. The EPPP is offered on a network composed of more than 320 Prometric Technology Centers located in Canada, the United States, and its territories.

What to Expect at the Computer Testing Centers

Computer testing centers are built to standard specifications and vary primarily on the basis of size. Private modular workstations provide workspace, comfortable seating, and proper lighting. Proctors monitor the testing process through an observation window and from within the testing room. Parabolic mirrors mounted on the walls assist proctors in observing the testing process. All testing sessions are videotaped and audio monitored. During the testing session, people taking examinations other than the EPPP may be working in the testing room. Some of these other examinations will be of the same multiple-choice format as the EPPP, whereas other examinations may require test-takers to type essays.

Computer knowledge is not required to take a computerized examination. Before the examination begins, a simple introductory lesson (tutorial) is presented that explains the process of selecting answers and moving from question to question. The time candidates spend on the practice lesson does not count against the time allotted for the examination. Most candidates take approximately 5 to 10 minutes to complete the tutorial and may repeat it, if desired. Candidates may select their answers using either the keyboard or the mouse. Candidates are strongly encouraged to use the tutorial prior to taking the examination. During the tutorial, candidates will learn how they can skip forward or backward through the examination and review questions. Candidates should be sure they understand how to review questions when they take the tutorial.

The testing software contains a feature that allows candidates to mark questions that they might wish to review later, if time permits. Any question can be marked, regardless of whether it has been left blank or answered. Questions can be reviewed whether or not they have been marked. It is not necessary to unmark a question in order for it to be scored at the end of the examination.

Candidates are allowed to make scratch notes on material supplied by the testing center. This material consists of plastic-coated white boards and erasable pens. Candidates are not allowed to bring in their own scratch paper. The white boards are collected by testing center staff at the completion of the examination. Scratch material is given to candidates only on request. It is not automatically supplied. Candidates are also allowed to use earplugs or headphones that are supplied by the testing center, or they may bring their own. Earplugs or headphones are not automatically distributed to candidates. Candidates must ask testing center staff for them. However, because the testing centers do not guarantee the availability of these devices, candidates who believe that they will need earplugs or headphones are strongly advised to bring their own. Earplugs or headphones brought by candidates are subject to inspection by testing center staff.

The testing centers are fully accessible and compliant with the Americans With Disabilities Act. For information about how to request reasonable accommodations, candidates must contact the licensing authority of the jurisdiction in which they are seeking licensure prior to applying to take the examination. Candidates must submit appropriate documentation of their request for accommodations to the licensing authority of the jurisdiction in which they are seeking licensure, at the time that they submit their initial application materials. Only those candidates who have been granted approval from their licensing authority will receive reasonable accommodations during testing.

What Is the Evidence That the Exam Is Valid?

It is not possible to conduct certain types of validity studies on a high-stakes exam such as the EPPP for practical and ethical reasons. Nor is it possible to do a predictive validity study by licensing 1,000 candidates who score below the cut-score and then compare them with a matched sample who pass on some multidimensional assessment of competence. It is possible, however, to look at correlates of exam scores and derive some evidence of concurrent validity.

As a high-stakes licensing exam for which protection of the public is intended, the EPPP follows psychometric practices for licensing exams that have come to be applied across many professions. In part these practices are embedded in a history of legislative mandates and legal case findings and precedents regarding test appropriateness, usage, and fairness. The overall process of establishing content validity, as described in the *Standards for Educational and Psychological Testing* (American Educational Research Association [AERA], American Psychological Association [APA], & National Council on Measurement in Education [NCME], 1999) emphasizes the need to conduct a practice analysis to ensure that the knowledge, skills, or abilities assessed in credentialing initiatives are limited to those required for competent performance and that they serve a public protection function. According to contemporary theorists such as Messick (1989, 1995), content validity is one aspect of a comprehensive theory of construct validity. From Messick's perspective, the meaning and interpretation of test scores is established on the basis of many different types of empirical investigations, of which a practice analysis is but one example. Practice analyses for the EPPP have been conducted periodically to maintain the most current picture of the practice of psychology (Greenberg & DeJesuitus, 2003; Greenberg et al., 1996; Richman, 1982; Rosen & Mirone, 1986; Rosenfeld et al., 1983).

Additional content validation studies have been implemented by Smith (1984, 1985) to check on the clarity of the new content outline, the quality of the items, and the correspondence between the content categories in the test outline and the items. Further studies were conducted to provide an independent check that forms of the EPPP reflected the test specifications, and that the items were free of any unintended content bias with regard to ethnicity, gender, and age (Hambleton & Smith, 1988; Smith, Hambleton, & Rosen, 1988a, 1988b). A study by Smith and Greenberg (1998) was conducted to address selected recommendations made as part of an audit of the validity of the EPPP examination program conducted by the State of California (Werner, 1989), resulting in an elaboration and enhancement of the test specification document.

How Do Students Prepare for the Examination for Professional Practice in Psychology?

A number of resources are available to licensure candidates in preparing for the EPPP. To begin with, although the exam is intended to protect the public by assuring a minimal level of knowledge, it is also assumed that the well-prepared student should be able to pass the exam and proceed to licensure and practice. For many students a review of their own graduate course notes is sufficient to study in their area of specialty. Because the exam is generic to all areas of professional practice in psychology, it may also be advisable to read a basic text in areas of practice to which the student has not been exposed. For example, a clinical student might want to review an I/O text or a school psychology text.

A valuable set of resources is available from the ASPPB. The ASPPB Web site has an "Information for Candidates" brochure describing the exam and the exam structure and topics covered. It also contains details on how to obtain a publication entitled *Items From Previous Exams*. It contains 250 items used on past versions of the EPPP and an answer key and reference list. Exam items that are included span the content outline and are intended to give candidates for licensure or certification a sense of what EPPP items are like. Other information of interest on the ASPPB Web site includes data on the average performance of students from graduate programs across the country, and licensure requirements of different states and provinces. ASPPB also offers a practice exam that can be taken at Prometric sites to acquaint the candidate with the workings of the computerized test site.

Commercial test preparation companies advertise regularly in APA publications. They offer test study materials, review workshops, and practice tests. Several Web sites can also be found on the Internet

Primary Method of Preparation for the Examination for Professional Practice in Psychology

Method	n	Percent	Mean scaled score
ASPPB items from previous examinations	181	4.3	518.43
ASPPB practice examination	301	7.1	513.68
Commercially sponsored workshop or materials	2,024	47.6	574.54
Individual study	606	14.3	537.88
Informal group sessions	120	2.8	569.39
Professionally sponsored workshop or materials	544	12.8	519.90
None	10	0.2	424.10
No response	463	10.9	517.35

Note. ASPPB = Association of State and Provincial Psychology Boards.

offering study materials, online workshops, and other materials. All of these are independent of ASPPB, and ASPPB does not sanction any of them. ASPPB cautions that item theft is a violation of copyright law and an ethical breach that may jeopardize the license of anyone who is caught passing on test items for sale or otherwise.

Along with demographic data, exam takers are asked for some information on how they prepared for the exam. Table 4.3 identifies the primary method of test preparation for candidates who took the test between August 31, 2003 and July 31, 2004. Table 4.4 presents the estimated amount of time spent preparing for the EPPP by the same candidates.

Note that the group members with the highest exam scores are those who took the commercially sponsored workshops. Note also that there is a direct correspondence between number of hours of test preparation and mean test score. Remember, however, that correlation does not prove causation, and it may be that the most conscientious students may do the most preparing and may also have studied harder as graduate students.

Estimated Time Spent Preparing for the Examination for Professional Practice in Psychology

Preparation	n	Percent	Mean scaled score
None	4	0.1	361.00
Less than 50 hours	112	2.6	446.65
50–99 hours	555	13.1	520.75
100–199 hours	1,119	26.3	560.51
200 or more hours	1,733	40.8	561.84
No response	726	17.1	538.33

TABLE 4.5

Years Since Completion of the Degree on Which Application Is Based

Number of years	*n*	Percent	Mean scaled score
0–1 year	1,615	38.0	579.00
2–3 years	1,752	41.2	554.33
4–5 years	426	10.0	493.60
6–7 years	186	4.4	473.53
8–9 years	72	1.7	502.88
10–14 years	79	1.9	468.37
15–19 years	39	0.9	416.49
20 or more years	45	1.1	485.16
No response	35	0.8	465.23

Table 4.5 shows the relationship between test scores and the number of years since completion of the degree on which the application for licensure is based. It is tempting to say take the test as soon as you are eligible, but again it is not possible to know what caused people to take the exam several years later.

What Does the Future Hold for the EPPP?

The EPPP has undergone many changes since its inception. From an exam based on a logical analysis of the field of professional practice, the EPPP has developed into an exam with an empirically based structure reflecting the practice of professional psychology in the United States and Canada. From twice annual paper-and-pencil administrations at one or two locations in a jurisdiction, the exam is now available continuously on computer 5 or 6 days per week, in locations convenient to most candidates. Items are now pretested, virtually eliminating the need to occasionally double key an item when a candidate has made a valid argument that one of the alternates could also be correct. The exam is available in a French bilingual format and many adaptations can be made for disabled candidates.

The EPPP and the process by which it is constructed will continue to undergo development and refinement. Currently more systematic ways of developing items are being explored. The computer format allows for new item formats. It is possible to include video vignettes in items, or to have branching items that take the candidate along several steps of a decision tree. The exam now is administered in the same form as paper-and-pencil exams, with the computer acting as an electronic page turner, but more sophisticated formats are possible in the future. Computer constructed testing involves having the computer create an individual test for each examinee according to the test specifications. Computer adaptive testing asks harder questions if the examinee gets an item right and easier if the item is answered wrong, until it can determine the examinee's performance level or make a pass–fail decision. These formats are expensive and can require huge item banks. It is likely that it will be a number of years before they are incorporated in the EPPP.

References

American Educational Research Association, American Psychological Association, & National Council on Measurement in Education. (1999). *Standards for educational and psychological testing.* Washington DC: American Educational Research Association.

Bloom, B., Englehart, M., Furst, E., Hill, W., & Krathwohl, D. (1956). *Taxonomy of educational objectives: The classification of educational goals. Handbook I: Cognitive domain.* New York and Toronto: Longmans, Green.

Greenberg, S., & DeJesuitus, L. (2003). *Study of the practice of licensed psychologists in the United States and Canada* (for the Association of State and Provincial Psychology Boards). New York: Professional Examination Service.

Greenberg, S., Smith, I. L., & Muenzen, P. M. (1996). *Study of the practice of licensed psychologists in the United States and Canada* (for the Association of State and Provincial Psychology Boards). New York: Professional Examination Service.

Haladyna, T. M. (1999). *Developing and validating multiple-choice test items* (2nd ed.) Mahwah, NJ: Erlbaum.

Haladyna, T. M., Downing, S. M., & Rodriquez, M. C. (2002). A review of multiple-choice item writing guidelines for classroom assessment. *Applied Measurement in Education, 15,* 309–333.

Hambleton, R. K., & Smith, I. L. (1988). *Content validity and fairness review of the 1987 forms of the Examination for Professional Practice in Psychology* (final report). New York: Professional Examination Service.

Messick, S. (1989). Validity. In R. L. Linn (Ed.), *Educational measurement* (3rd ed., pp. 13–103). New York: Macmillan.

Messick, S. (1995). Validity of psychological assessment: Validation of inferences from persons' responses and performances as scientific inquiry into score meaning. *American Psychologist, 50,* 741–749.

Richman, S. (1982). *The role delineation study for the Examination for Professional Practice in Psychology* (final report). New York: Professional Examination Service.

Rosen, G. A., & Mirone, J. A. (1986). *The test specification revision project for the Examination for Professional Practice in Psychology* (final report). New York: Professional Examination Service.

Rosenfeld, M., Shimberg, B., & Thornton, R. F. (1983). *Job analysis of licensed psychologists in the United States and Canada.* Princeton, NJ: Educational Testing Service.

Smith, I. L. (1984). *Content validity study of the EPPP item bank.* New York: Professional Examination Service.

Smith, I. L. (1985). Content validity study of the AASPB item bank. *Professional Practice of Psychology, 6,* 233–250.

Smith, I. L., & Greenberg, S. (1998). Defining constructs underlying the practice of psychology in the United States and Canada. In A. S. Bellack, M. Hersen (Series Eds.), & A. N. Wiens (Vol. Ed.), *Comprehensive clinical psychology: Vol. 2. Professional issues* (pp. 121–135). Oxford, England: Elsevier.

Smith, I. L., Hambleton, R. K., & Rosen, G. A. (1988a). Content validity investigations of the Examination for Professional Practice in Psychology. *Professional Practice of Psychology, 9,* 43–80.

Smith, I. L., Hambleton, R. K., & Rosen, G. A. (1988b, August). *Content validity studies of the Examination for Professional Practice in Psychology.* Paper presented at the 96th Annual Convention of the American Psychological Association, Atlanta, GA.

Werner, E. (1989). *Analysis of the validity of the Examination for Professional Practice of Psychology.* Sacramento: California Department of Consumer Affairs.

William T. Melnyk and Karen S. Vaughn

Complementary Examinations

5

M any members of licensing boards, as well as some researchers over the years (Hill, 1984; Novy, Kopel, & Swank, 1996; Wand, Hess, & Madrid, 1982) have held that there needed to be ways to evaluate a candidate's readiness for practice in addition to the Examination for Professional Practice in Psychology (EPPP; see chap. 4, this volume). The theory was that a multiple-choice examination, even though carefully designed, validated, and administered, could not in and of itself assess knowledge of an individual jurisdiction's statutes or the subtleties of applying content knowledge to the complex human interaction required for therapeutic interventions. Even though the EPPP has become the standard assessment criteria for entry into the profession, additional examinations are used by many of the licensing and regulatory bodies in the United States and Canada. These additional and complementary examinations have been developed at the state or provincial level rather than the standardized format of the EPPP. Hence, there is wide variance in whether complementary exams are required as well as within the format and administration of these exams. Hill, a former president of the Association of State and Provincial Psychology Boards (ASPPB), wrote an article entitled "Oral Examinations: Standards and Strategies" (1984) in the *Journal of Professional Practice in Psychology*. She strongly recommended that boards should develop structured oral examinations based on the results of job analyses similar to the ones done by ASPPB in 1978 and 1984. It is important to keep in mind that licensing and regulatory boards are charged with determining the best possible way to protect the public when the provision of psychological services is concerned. "Oral examinations in psychology were developed to identify those who have mastered, at an acceptable entry level, the skills necessary for minimal competency so that the public may be protected against unsafe practice" (Novy et al., 1996, pp. 23–24).

The potential combinations of exam requirements can be (a) EPPP only; (b) EPPP and written jurisprudence exam; (c) EPPP and oral jurisprudence exam; (d) EPPP, written jurisprudence, and oral examination; (e) EPPP and an oral interview; or (f) EPPP, written jurisprudence, and an oral interview or exam. Sixty-one of the 62 ASPPB member jurisdictions require the EPPP. Quebec requires the exam only for candidates who apply for licensure outside of the province. According to the ASPPB (2004) *Handbook on Licensing and Credentialing* (as of 2005), member jurisdictions report that in addition to the EPPP, 48 jurisdictions require a jurisprudence examination, 31 require an oral examination or interview, and 7 report that they require both oral examinations and written jurisprudence exams. As will be explained in greater detail within the discussion of current trends, it is important to check current jurisdictional requirements as these are changing.

This chapter presents information on types, rationale, and development of complementary examinations that may be required of a licensure candidate. We offer resource information to investigate requirements and preparation for these exams as well as discuss the current trends pertaining to the examination of candidates.

Oral Examinations

Oral examinations are used extensively in psychology and in many other professions. In medicine, they are often used as part of the selection process for entry to a medical school along with the MCAT examination. They are used to assess candidates for specialty certification by medical specialty boards. In university psychology departments they are used for comprehensive examinations and for the defense of theses. They are used by many licensing boards as part of the certification process, and are required by the ASPPB for both of their mobility vehicles: the Certificate of Professional Qualification (CPQ) and the reciprocity agreements among licensing boards in the United States and Canada. However, as of June 1, 2006, passage of an oral examination will no longer be a requirement for obtaining the CPQ (see chap. 9, this volume).

The ABPP uses oral exams as part of the process to determine specialty designation. In spite of the very broad use in many professions, the use of oral examinations by psychology boards in the past 5 years has been called into serious doubt by some states.

Many psychology boards in the United States and Canada require an oral examination as part of the procedure for licensing an individual for the independent practice of psychology. The purpose of the oral examination is usually stated as measuring the ability to exercise sound reasoning and judgment in the integration and application of the knowledge of psychological science, practice methods, ethics, and legal–regulatory mandates. The oral exam is intended to measure the application of both theoretical and applied knowledge to clinical issues and problems. The procedures used range from unstructured interviews to fully structured oral examinations. Structured examinations are considered to be the most reliable form of oral examination and are usually centered on a standardized vignette, which is followed by predetermined questions presented in a standard format so that every examinee receives the same experience. Examiners may range from current board members, past board members, practicing psychologists whom a board determines are experts in practice areas, to those psychologists simply willing to serve as examiners. Most licensing boards provide training to their examiners to improve reliability.

About half of the 62 member jurisdictions of the ASPPB do not administer an oral examination. In 2004, 27 states in the United States and 9 provinces in Canada (by 2005) used oral examinations for licensing. In Canada, national mobility agreements require all provinces and territories to use an oral examination as part of the licensing process. The reasons given by boards for omitting this part of the licensing process usually focus on the fear that the procedure can be subjective and seen as unfair or not defensible when challenged in court. In fact, some state legislatures have forbidden the use of these examinations. Challenges in Canada have been nonexistent because, in general, litigation on such matters is less common. However, in spite of this concern, the legal challenges to oral examinations have been largely unsuccessful. It is perhaps ironic and somewhat surprising that some of the largest states (e.g., New York and California) have stopped using oral examinations for certification. With large budgets, these states are often the most capable of developing defensible orals. Good orals are very costly to develop and administer. Other states, like California, have based their decision on psychometric review and analyses leading to the conclusion that oral examinations cannot be made to be reliable and valid, and that they add very little to the assessment process for entry into the profession of psychology and do not enhance the ability of the board to protect the public. There is great conflict and controversy surrounding the use of the oral examination. What message is given to graduate students when it is concluded that it is difficult if not impossible to administer a fair oral? No movement has been observed toward a decision to drop comprehensive and thesis orals in graduate schools of psychology. It is ironic that for entry into specialties for medicine as well as psychology in both the United States and Canada, the oral examination process is used, and that often psychologists are hired as the most capable professionals to make these exams reliable and valid.

HISTORY AND RATIONALE OF ORAL EXAMINATIONS

The first survey on the use of oral examinations was conducted in 1980 by a committee of the American Association of State Psychology Boards (AASPB), now the ASPPB. The results of this survey were published in a manual, *Committee on Oral Examination Procedures: Guidelines for Conducting Oral Examinations* (1982). Among the conclusions of the 1982 ASPPB guidelines were that the content of oral examinations be related to studies of the EPPP.

Hill (1984) suggested that a job analysis be conducted to develop the content domains for oral exams and to provide a rationale that the skills and knowledge measured by the oral examination are necessary for competent performance at a minimal level. She further indicated that multiple-choice exams such as the EPPP do not lend themselves to testing the ability to make complex deductions and inferences, measure decision-making skills, or assess oral communication skills. All of these are important to the practice of psychology and can be more readily measured by an oral exam. Hill concluded her article by recommending that ASPPB develop a uniform oral examination to supplement the EPPP.

The ASPPB *Manual on Oral Examinations for Licensing or Certification* (ASPPB, 1986), stated that the format of the oral examination can be structured, semistructured, or unstructured. Although the structured examination was seen as reducing flexibility and spontaneous interaction, it increases reliability through consistency and makes the calculation of interexaminer reliability possible. The manual, as well as the subsequent guidelines published by ASPPB, were developed as a resource for licensing boards who wished to include the oral examination in their licensing requirements.

In 1997, the ASPPB Committee on Education and Training for Credentialing was asked to review the oral examination process and to develop a set of guidelines to be used by member boards in the United States and Canada. As a first step, jurisdictions were surveyed to determine the extent and the kind of oral examination usage. A high response rate (55 out of 61 jurisdictions) suggested a strong continued interest in oral examinations. The majority of the 34 jurisdictions that used oral examinations in 1997 administered jurisprudence or some form of competency examinations.

Despite the support for the utility of the oral examination and despite concerns regarding its lack of standardization, reliability, and validity as well as the need for improvement, little jurisdictional research was spawned by the early ASPPB formal recognition of the exam's importance. By 1997 only three jurisdictions had published data regarding the interrater reliability of their exams (Edwards, 1984; Novy et al., 1996; Watson, 1984). This lack of published data would later be one of the main bases for challenges to the oral exam and fear of litigation by many of the licensing boards who already administer them or were considering inclusion of the oral.

However, utilization of an oral examination gained support and was assisted in growth by the mobility efforts. One of the chapter authors remembers from the early developmental meetings toward establishing reciprocity the consensus that face-to-face interview, at the very least, was important in determining acceptance of a licensed psychologist from another jurisdiction. The strong feeling was that the public could not be best served by "paper only licensing." Just as it appeared that the oral examination was building toward being more the standard than the exception, momentum began to build against its use, based primarily on the difficulty in proving reliability and concerns about validity. Fueling these difficulties was the reality that most licensing boards did not have the financial or personnel resources to conduct the needed research and development.

In their June 1999 newsletter, the Arizona Board of Psychologist Examiners announced that the oral examination would no longer be required for licensure. The reason for this decision was because of the fact that following a review of the oral with the expert help of persons such as Norman Hertz, manager of the Office of Examination Resources of the State of California, it was decided that improvement of the examination was beyond the financial and personnel resources of the board.

CURRENT TRENDS

On November 2, 2001, the California Board of Psychology voted to discontinue the use of oral examinations and replace them with a written test, the California Jurisprudence and Professional Ethics

Examination. The oral examination in California had undergone extensive development and improvement since its inception in 1990. It had been widely recognized as the best examination given by any psychology regulatory board in the United States and Canada. Nevertheless, assisted by the expert help of Norman Hertz and by an external expert from the RAND Corporation, a comprehensive review of the oral examination procedures was conducted by the board. Among the conclusions, the board reported that although the oral portion contained well-developed content validity based on various ASPPB practice analyses, the examination contained a serious source of error because of the different interpretations of the content provided by the oral examiners. Tough examiners coupled with tough questions could spell doom for the candidate and create false negative decisions. Other considerations of reliability and validity led to the conclusion that the oral examination did not meet the current standards for testing (e.g., American Educational Research Association, American Psychological Association, & National Council on Measurement in Education, 1999). It is likely that this decision by California will set the stage for other states and provinces to reconsider the use of oral examinations. It is also likely that the comprehensive and thorough review of what appeared to be the best oral examination in North America will give rise to further legal challenges of the oral exam.

The challenges following the action by the California Board of Psychology are already evident. In New Mexico, in March 2003, a group of psychologists, some of whom had failed the oral examination, began legal action against the Board of Psychologist Examiners. They hired Norman Hertz from California to review the examination (Hertz, 2003). He published his report in May, and concluded that the oral examination did not meet current standards.

In a personal communication from Gloria Carrillo (June 28, 2004), an administrator for the New Mexico Board of Psychologist Examiners, to W. T. Melnyk, one of the authors of this chapter, this challenge was confirmed but stated that no court action had occurred. The board hired its own consultant who worked with them for a year to improve the examination. Special attention was given to the training of the oral examiners and to the scoring procedures. The oral examination was retained.

In a communication of the ASPPB's electronic mailing list (July 23, 2004), Len Tamura of the Colorado Board of Psychologist Examiners reported that the state went through a sunset review and the oral examination was eliminated. The exam now is prohibited by statute. The examination in Colorado was very good, and a lot of time and money was spent to make it one of the best in the United States.

The Texas State Board of Examiners of Psychologists Web site (2005) indicates that they have undergone a sunset review. Although the Sunset Advisory Commission recommended that the oral examination for candidates for licensure be discontinued, it was kept, and a panel was appointed to reevaluate the Texas oral exam and recommend changes that should be made to the oral examination process in that jurisdiction.

Oral examinations can be troubling for a board of examiners in psychology and poor examinations may leave a board vulnerable to charges of arbitrariness or unfairness. Every attempt must be made to assure that the examination is reliable and valid. The oral should be undertaken only for good reason. Licensing can have economic value for those seeking to become licensed, and due process must be accorded to those who fail.

In 1996, at the request of member boards, ASPPB lawyers conducted a search of the literature to determine the legal challenges to oral examinations. There have been few challenges to date of oral examinations in psychology or in any other professions. None of the challenges have been successful. Claims that orals are administered arbitrarily and capriciously and that they are inherently unfair have been dismissed by the courts.

By 2005, there still had been no successful challenges of the oral examination process used by psychology boards. The oral remains the most effective way to measure the ability to apply knowledge and skills in the clinical environment. However, the psychometric reviews of the orals given in California and New Mexico by Norman Hertz, one of the foremost experts in this field, should be cause for concern.

The information in this section has been taken from the ASPPB oral examination guidelines (August, 1999) as well as from the authors' experience. These guidelines were accepted at the 1999 Annual Meeting of the ASPPB Member Boards and were recommended for use by Psychology Regulatory Boards who wanted to produce defensible orals. They can be accessed at the ASPPB Web site (http://www.asppg.org).

RELIABILITY AND VALIDITY CONSIDERATIONS

Much of the criticism of the oral has been related to difficulty with reliability and validity. To be defensible and fair, the oral examination must be reliable. Some of the ways to achieve reliability include use of a structured format, consensus-based protocols, extensive training of examiners, consistency of examination procedures, case vignettes, and structured scoring and reporting procedures. One of the more practical ways to make the examination reliable is to have the content repeatable across examinees by using a consistent format. The consistent format allows each examinee to be examined using exactly the same structure and scoring methods.

In terms of its validity, most studies of the oral have advocated content validity. Content validity should be based on a job analysis (e.g., *Study of the Practice of Licensed Psychologists in United States and Canada*, ASPPB, 1995, and revalidated in 2004) and recognized standards for training (e.g., American Psychological Association and the Canadian Psychological Association Accreditation Standards). The ASPPB practice analysis contains the results of a survey sent to approximately 7,500 psychologists in the United States and Canada. It was developed to identify the roles and responsibilities performed by new and experienced licensed psychologists in different areas of practice. The purpose of the practice analysis was to update the items on the ASPPB written exam, the EPPP. The return rate on this survey was 60%. The analysis produced information about the demographic background and training of licensed psychologists, the critical and core knowledge they use in practice, and qualitative comments about the short- and long-range changes occurring in the practice of the profession. The use of the roles and responsibilities, as defined in the practice analysis, are recommended to develop the content for an oral examination. These roles and responsibilities were confirmed in a ministudy done by ASPPB and the Professional Examination Service in 2004 (W. T. Melnyk, personal communication, February 10, 2006). The four key roles identified by this analysis were direct service, outreach and consultation, academic preparation, and professional development. Each role had a list of associated responsibilities and activities. The direct service role as defined in the practice analysis was rated by the respondents in the survey as the most important for practice and the most important for the protection of the public from harm. More than 70% of practice time was spent in this role.

CONTENT OF THE ORAL EXAM

The responsibilities and activities related to the direct service role are clearly defined and have been used to determine the content of the ASPPB oral examination. They are as follows: define problems; observe and interview effectively; assess client, patient, and organizational needs; diagnose and formulate problems accurately; design, implement, and evaluate interventions; gather information from related sources; make appropriate referrals; follow professional and ethical standards and guidelines; follow state, provincial, and national laws and regulations. One method of assessing these abilities is to measure each skill in relation to a standardized case vignette that presents a general, generic scenario followed by a standardized format of questions. This method can be used to address both reliability and validity issues. The use of a generic case vignette addresses validity; the standardized format in which each examinee answers the same basic questions addresses reliability. The content of the questions is related to the practice analysis, and this provides content validity.

Examination Format

Each examination on a case vignette is usually organized in the same format. The common eight sections that have been derived by the ASPPB (1986) Committee on Oral Examination Guidelines from the direct service role of the practice analysis are as follows:

- identifies problems and diagnosis;
- assessment and evaluation;
- treatment planning, implementation, and outcome assessment;
- crisis evaluation, treatment, and management;
- human diversity;
- professional ethics and standards;
- legal and regulatory mandates; and
- professional limitations and judgment.

THE CASE VIGNETTE

Given that most psychology licenses are generic, case vignettes will typically describe clients and patients who would be familiar to most practitioners. Case vignettes are written to describe clients and patients experiencing common psychological disorders such as depression, anxiety, adjustment disorders, and so forth. Each case vignette describes the client and patient demographically (e.g., age, sex, ethnicity, socioeconomic status, occupation, education, marital status, and family configuration), the presenting problem or problems, and relevant history (social, developmental, medical, family, career, educational, etc.). As the examination proceeds, further prepared details may be added to the vignette including formal test results, a crisis situation, a cultural diversity change in the demographic information, and legal and ethical issues to consider. Some states such as California, which adopted most of the procedures suggested by ASPPB, used the results of a single psychological test in their vignette presentation (e.g., the Minnesota

Multiphasic Personality Inventory). In other jurisdictions, the examinee may be allowed to choose his or her own instrument, and explain and justify its use.

Some jurisdictions have developed a pool of vignettes more specifically geared to a candidate's stated specialty and are chosen to relate to that specialty. For example, this approach avoids a scenario in which an industrial/organizational psychology candidate might be presented with a child clinical vignette.

SAMPLE VIGNETTE FOR STANDARD ORAL EXAMINATION

> Janet is a 34-year-old woman who self-referred to you for counseling. She has recently returned to school to complete her BA degree, and she is feeling overwhelmed by all her responsibilities. Janet was divorced 3 years ago and has custody of her two children, a girl 8 and a boy 6. The children's father left the state after the divorce and remarried. He is erratic with child support and seldom sees or talks with his children. Janet has been working as a receptionist since the divorce but wants to complete her degree to qualify for a better paying job.
>
> She came in to see you because she has been having difficulty sleeping, feels exhausted, and is unable to control feelings of sadness and tearfulness. She reported that last week she burst into tears when her supervisor at work criticized her for misplacing a message. She has been short-tempered with her children and fears that she may be hurting them with her anger. The children's teachers have told her that both children are creating discipline problems in school. She reports still feeling a great deal of anger toward her ex-husband for abandoning the family.
>
> Janet feels that her life is miserable and empty. She cannot remember the last time she had fun. She reported with embarrassment that her job, school, and children all feel like burdens, and she often feels like running away. She feels desperate.

The preceding is an example of a typical vignette. Approximately 12 questions are asked, covering the previously mentioned eight content areas. Test data is provided to give the examinees the opportunity to elaborate on their knowledge of assessment and ability to integrate material (ASPPB, 1982).

SCORING

Table 5.1 presents the ASPPB recommended scoring criteria and descriptions of the basis of scores obtained for which the candidates will be rated in each of the eight content areas. The following is a more specific outline of scoring criteria for the first direct service role taken from the *Oral Examination Guidelines* (ASPPB, 1999, pp. 53–69):

TABLE 5.1

ASPPB Scoring Criteria and Descriptions in Eight Content Areas

Type	Rating	Description
Incompetent	0	Commits errors of omission that result in active danger to client.
Highly ineffective	1	Demonstrates lack of knowledge, makes repeated errors, and commits errors of omission that result in a passive danger to client.
Ineffective	2	Makes minor errors; does not quite address issues.
Effective	3	Demonstrates minimal competence for safe practice, can practice independently, has knowledge of core areas of practice, and consults if necessary.
Highly effective	4	Demonstrates skills that are above minimum competence, demonstrates breadth of knowledge with depth in limited areas.
Exceptional	5	Demonstrates exceptional depth and breadth of knowledge in all areas within the content areas.

I. Identifies Problems and Diagnosis

Superior

- Clearly, concisely, and comprehensively develops and articulates possible diagnoses;
- demonstrates a sophisticated understanding of how multiple factors affect biological and psychological functioning;
- demonstrates comprehensive knowledge of diagnostic systems and criteria;
- presents an exceptional understanding of biological, psychological, social, and cultural factors when providing a diagnosis;
- clearly integrates variety of relevant data in reaching empirically based and theoretically consistent differential diagnoses;
- cites relevant personality theories that describe the etiology of atypical behaviors within a behavioral disorder;
- supports or rules out one or more diagnoses by integrating data from multiple sources with other information into a coherent whole (e.g., genetic factors, physical symptoms, demographic distribution, comorbidity); and
- comprehensively integrates human diversity factors with diagnosis, if appropriate.

Acceptable

- Demonstrates working knowledge of *Diagnostic and Statistical Manual of Mental Disorders (DSM)* diagnostic criteria;
- offers consistent theoretical rationale for inclusion and exclusion of possible diagnoses;
- effectively develops and articulates diagnoses;
- discusses how symptoms common to several diagnoses are part of a differential diagnosis;
- considers epidemiology and potential genetic components when rendering diagnoses;
- integrates client data (e.g., psychological, biological, social) when formulating a diagnosis that is consistent with information and that rules our competing diagnoses;
- provides a theoretical base that incorporates information (e.g., clinical, medical, social, educational, familial, etc.) to support the diagnoses and rule out alternative diagnoses; and
- some integration of human diversity factors into diagnoses, if appropriate.

Questionable

- Fails to describe rationale for inclusion and exclusion of possible diagnoses;
- questionable ability to identify presenting problems;
- little or no integration of human diversity factors in developing diagnoses, when appropriate;
- overlooks factors in diagnosis;
- recognizes potential for misdiagnosis by relying on current diagnostic trends but does not clearly relate this to the case;
- presents diagnostic options but does not clearly relate them to the case;
- states how diagnosis can be supported by symptomatology but incompletely incorporates relevant data;
- demonstrates questionable ability to identify or overlooks key presenting problems; and
- deals with relevant theoretical framework in a questionable manner.

Unqualified

- Diagnostic skills inadequate to lead to differential diagnoses;
- does not know diagnostic categories or criteria;
- shows limited ability to rule out competing diagnoses;
- considers only a single diagnostic possibility when others are clearly relevant;

- identifies probable diagnoses without linking to supporting data;
- failure to consider human diversity factors, when appropriate;
- focuses on irrelevant data; and
- demonstrates skills which are inadequate to lead to a differential diagnosis.

Incompetent

- Misdiagnoses based on a misinterpretation of *DSM* multiaxial classification system;
- fails to notice or evaluate psychological problems;
- fails to focus on the key presenting symptoms or issues;
- diagnoses presence of a personality disorder without sufficient supporting information;
- fails to make differential diagnoses or note possibilities;
- diagnoses psychological symptoms without considering potential medical explanations;
- diagnoses inconsistent with available data or seriously misdiagnoses the problem(s);
- prejudges the case;
- demonstrates bias in problem definition and conceptualization;
- presents a significant danger to client in terms of erroneous diagnosis;
- violates community standards of practice; and
- stereotypical prejudicial use of human diversity factors in making diagnosis.

The ASPPB *Oral Examination Guidelines* include additional details on the following topics: conduct of the oral examination, examinee's orientation handbook, oral examiners' administrative procedures handbook, selection of examiners, and training of examiners. They also contain other materials that can be used to develop an oral examination. These materials may be helpful in terms of what to expect from the examination process.

To prepare for an oral examination it is recommended that the candidate access the ASPPB Web site at http://www.asppb.org. On the main page of the site, there is a quick link to Licensing Board Contact Info. This site gives the links for each state and provincial regulatory body. Specific information related to oral examinations will be available at these links (if an oral is required). It is also possible to search the *Handbook of Licensing and Credentialing* on the Web site to obtain contact information for the boards that administer oral exams. Because many jurisdictions are following the ASPPB *Oral Examination Guidelines*, it would be useful to read these as they can be downloaded in pdf-readable format from the ASPPB Web site. It is important to keep in mind that these are the recommended guidelines, which means that the jurisdiction to which one is applying may use a different exam, format, or a variation of the guidelines. Therefore, it is essential that the board be contacted to directly obtain information specific to their oral examination and recommended study materials.

Jurisprudence Examinations

The word *jurisprudence* derives from the Latin term *juris prudentia*, which means "the study, knowledge, or science of law." In the United States, jurisprudence commonly means the philosophy of law.

The purpose of a jurisprudence examination is to assess the understanding and knowledge of (a) professional conduct and ethical principles and (b) the legislative provisions relevant to the practice of psychology in the state or province. Knowledge assessed includes statutory and case laws, regulations, standards of practice, codes of ethics, and ethical guidelines. A jurisprudence examination is required by 48 of the 62 state and provincial licensing boards. Even if a candidate has met one of the mobility requirements as listed by ASPPB (see chap. 9), a state or provincial board can require a jurisprudence examination to practice in that jurisdiction to assure that the incoming psychologist was knowledgeable about the laws and regulations before practicing in that state or province. The exam can be part of an oral examination, administered as an oral exam on its own, or given in written form, usually as a multiple-choice exam. The most common pass point is 70%. This information can be found on the ASPPB Web site (http://www.asppb.org/) under the heading *Handbook on Licensing and Credentialing*. This handbook is updated on a regular basis and gives the licensing requirements for all states and provinces. Some jurisdictions will give the number of questions pertaining to each set of regulations and acts and statutes. An example of the type of knowledge required in a jurisprudence examination is as follows: confidentiality (obligations, limitations), consent to treatment, access to records and information, release information, reporting obligations, proper recordkeeping, and professional conduct. Because jurisdictions may vary in some of their laws pertaining to these or other content areas, it is essential to study the specific statutes of a licensing jurisdiction. Each state and province provides the candidate for licensure a list of materials to use for preparation.

It would be virtually impossible to give a brief history of the jurisprudence examination as was presented in the section pertaining to oral exams. The jurisprudence exams administered by licensing boards were developed from individual jurisdiction's laws, and it would be difficult to ascertain when jurisprudence exams were instituted without surveying all 62 boards. From the authors' extensive experience with licensing boards, the primary reason for administering a jurisprudence exam is much like that of doctoral program professors who know that if they did not administer tests, their students would not prepare the material as well as when they do test over the material. In order for new licensees to be familiar with the laws of their state or province, they must read and be familiar with them. They must also be aware that these laws change periodically and that it is their responsibility to stay current with jurisdictional laws.

Because the knowledge areas examined are a matter of law or rule, there is less room for criticisms of interpretation, and therefore, the jurisprudence exam has not come under the scrutiny or been the subject of litigation as with the oral examination. Those exams that are in multiple-choice formats are more amenable to reliability and validity measures as well.

More varied than differences in laws and rules may be the differences in format of jurisprudence exams jurisdiction to jurisdiction. There does not appear to be any standardization or recommended format for these exams. As mentioned previously, some jurisprudence exams are administered orally, both to test the content knowledge and to serve as face-to-face contact with the applicant. Others are very content oriented, true vs. false, or multiple-choice format. Even in the multiple-choice format, some jurisdictions present case study examples, and candidates are to choose from the options presented.

To prepare for a jurisprudence examination, the candidate is urged to access the ASPPB Web site, find the link to the state or province of interest, and discover the information available about these examinations. For example, the Oklahoma Board of Examiners of Psychologists added their jurisprudence study material and guidelines to their Web site as others may have done as well (http://osbep.ok.gov).

It is also recommended that the board in the jurisdiction to which the candidate is applying for licensure be directly contacted about the materials required for preparation. Most boards will have copies available of relevant regulations, laws, and other necessary materials. Some will provide the address for purchasing these materials. Again, it is also possible to search the *Handbook of Licensing and Credentialing* on the ASPPB Web site to obtain contact information for the boards that administer jurisprudence exams. Board contact information for those administering jurisprudence exams may be obtained as well as passing score, format, and so forth.

Boards vary greatly in the amount of information about jurisprudence examinations that they provide on the Internet. Some mention only that the exam is given. Some say it is part of a broader oral examination. A few give excellent and detailed information about the examination. For example, the California Board of Psychology's Web site has a handbook for the *California Jurisprudence and Professional Ethics Examination*. It describes how the exam was developed, lists the study materials, and how these materials can be obtained. Similarly, the College of Psychologists of Ontario's Web site gives much detail on the requirements for the examination, the topics covered, and the percentage of the examination set aside for each topic. A list of the rules and regulations, standards of practice, laws, and so forth is given, along with information on how these may be obtained.

As important as obtaining the study materials and copies of statutes and rules is asking specific questions about the format of the jurisprudence exam. Is it a written exam or is it administered orally? Are case scenarios or vignettes presented? If it is written, is it multiple choice, true vs. false, short answer, or a combination? Is it pencil-and-paper or computerized? What is the pass point? Knowing the answers to these simple questions can help test takers to prepare for the exam and know what to expect.

Conclusion

As psychologists, we would rarely rely on one single measure to assess complex content and process variables. There has been continuing concern among many licensing bodies as well as researchers in the field of psychology about the use of the EPPP as the only measure of minimal competence to practice psychology independently. Many boards, to address this concern, have enlisted the support of their legislatures to include additional and complementary exams to more fully evaluate readiness to practice. However, some legislators have forbidden these additional examinations, claiming that they are unfair, unreliable, and invalid.

This chapter has outlined types of complementary examinations used by many licensing boards. We have attempted to explain the rationale for these exams and some of the difficulties with them. Although the procedures used by state and provincial psychology boards are often flawed, there have been few legal challenges. That could change. We have provided information about some of the current trends in the use of oral exams in particular. The California Board of Psychology (2001), who had what many have considered the best examination among psychology boards, has decided to eliminate the oral for psychometric reasons. This decision by the California Board of Psychology will very likely lead to more legal challenges for other boards in the future as lawyers become knowledgeable about the issues involved. The debate should be about whether or not the oral examination provides a useful component to the licensing process. For many jurisdictions in the United States and Canada, this is a firmly held conviction. The ASPPB guidelines go a long way toward helping to accomplish the goal of creating a fair, defensible, and useful exam. It is perhaps ironic that the most defensible oral examinations have been developed by psychologists, not for use in psychology, but for use by medical boards.

Jurisprudence exams are more widely used by licensing boards and have experienced less controversy and challenge. Licensing boards would probably more consistently agree on the importance of working knowledge of their state or provinces' statutes and rules as they pertain to responsible, ethical practice and protection of the public. It would seem logical that legislators would see the validity of practitioners being knowledgeable about their statutes, regulations, and rules, therefore yielding less resistance to this type of complementary examination.

Regardless of one's stance on the utility of these additional examinations, we encourage students to see them as opportunities to best prepare for sound ethical practice rather than just another hurdle to jump. If newly licensed psychologists have been assured through examination that they possess the ability to exercise sound reasoning and judgment in the integration and application of the knowledge of psychological science, practice methods, ethics, and legal–regulatory mandates, then they should feel more prepared to enter the practice of psychology.

References

American Educational Research Association, American Psychological Association, & National Council on Measurement in Education. (1999). *Standards for educational and psychological testing*. Washington, DC: American Educational Research Association.

Arizona Board of Psychology. (1999, June). Oral examinations no longer required by board. *News Letter, 3,* 1–2.

Association of State and Provincial Psychology Boards. (1982). *Committee on oral examination procedures: Guidelines for conducting oral examinations.* Montgomery, AL: Author.

Association of State and Provincial Psychology Boards. (1986). *The ASPPB manual on oral examinations for licensing or certification.* Montgomery, AL: Author.

Association of State and Provincial Psychology Boards. (1995). *Study of the practice of licensed psychologists in the United States and Canada.* Montgomery, AL: Author.

Association of State and Provincial Psychology Boards. (1999). *Oral examination guidelines.* Montgomery, AL: Author.

Association of State and Provincial Psychology Boards. (2004). *Handbook of licensing and certification requirements.* Retrieved February 10, 2006, from http://www.asppb.org/handbook/handbook

California Board of Psychology. (2001). *California jurisprudence and professional ethics examination.* Retrieved November 2, 2005, from http://www.psychboard.ca.gov/

Edwards, H. P. (1984). The Ontario model: The oral examination with invited examiners. *Professional Practice of Psychology, 5,* 94–102.

Hertz, N. R. (2003). *Evaluation of the oral examination of the New Mexico board of psychologist's examiners.* Folsom, CA: HZ Assessments.

Hill, D. S. (1984). Oral examinations: Standards and strategies. *Journal of Professional Practice in Psychology, 5,* 94–102.

Novy, D. M., Kopel, K. F., & Swank, P. R. (1996). Psychometrics of oral examinations for psychology licensure: The Texas examination as an example. *Professional Psychology: Research and Practice, 27*(4), 415–417.

Texas State Board of Examiners of Psychologists. (2005). *Texas State Board of Examiners of Psychologists.* Retrieved February 10, 2006, from http://www.tsbep.state.tx.us/

Wand, B., Hess, A., & Madrid, A. (1982). *Committee on oral examination procedures.* Montgomery, AL: Association of State and Provincial Psychology Boards.

Watson, M. A. (1984). The Colorado model: A structured oral examination. *Professional Practice of Psychology, 5,* 79–85.

Emil R. Rodolfa and W. Greg Keilin

Internship Training With Licensure on the Horizon

6

A student once told me that his faculty put up a conceptual wall at the point of internship. This student emphasized that there was no discussion of what to expect and no opportunity to understand and prepare for what would follow internship. This experience is not unusual for students completing their doctoral programs. This chapter attempts to reduce or remove that conceptual wall and highlight the significant issues involved in securing an internship, and provides suggestions to help students prepare for life after internship leading to licensure.

This chapter also provides an overview of the basic requirements for internship training, presents information about responding to problems during internship, and then discusses how experience accrued at an internship is related to supervised experience requirements by various state licensing boards. We offer suggestions about applying for internship and discuss the current status of the supply of and demand for internship slots. Our goal is to provide an overview of internship issues and an internship's relationship to licensure.

The Sequence of Training Leading to Licensure

A predoctoral internship is one element in the sequence of training leading to licensure. To become licensed, an individual must complete academic coursework, successfully accrue a certain number of practicum hours, complete an internship, and students in a doctorate of philosophy or some doctorate of psychology programs must write a dissertation, whereas most students in doctorate of psychology programs must complete a doctoral project rather than a dissertation. Each factor leads to graduation. Once an individual graduates, postdoctoral experience must be accrued. At some point in this process, either at graduation or on completion of all experience hours, each state requires a candidate for licensure to complete testing that will include the Examination for Professional Practice in Psychology (EPPP; see chap. 4, this volume) and perhaps a jurisprudence examination or an oral examination (see chap. 5, this volume). Once all requirements are completed, the individual will become licensed in one of the 50 states (see Figure 6.1).

AN INTERNSHIP DEFINED

The major difference between an internship and on-the-job supervised experience is that an internship provides an organized sequence of training that builds on academic knowledge. An internship allows an individual to continue receiving educational experiences while accruing supervised professional experience that will count toward licensure.

The Association of Psychology Postdoctoral and Internship Centers (APPIC) has specific membership criteria that define an internship (APPIC, 2004a, 2004c). These criteria emphasize the training nature of the internship experience, that it has to be organized and under the guidance of one individual (the director of training), and that multiple staff members must be available to act as role models and provide a variety of training experiences. APPIC standards maintain that there must be a minimum of two interns who each receive at least 2 hours of supervision and 2 hours of training on a weekly basis. They must be exposed to and participate in a variety of professional experiences, and at least 25% of an intern's time must be in face-to-face patient contact. The goal of these criteria is to ensure a balance between training and direct service experiences.

FIGURE 6.1

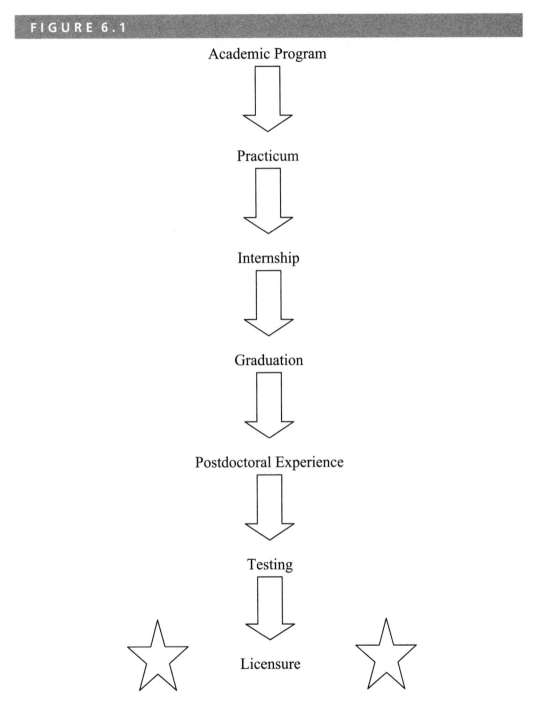

Sequence of education and training leading to licensure. Testing for licensure can occur at various points subsequent to the completion of the student's requirements for graduation. Testing will include one or more of the following: the Examination for Professional Practice in Psychology, an examination of state laws pertaining to the practice of psychology, or an oral examination or interview.

The Association of State and Provincial Psychology Boards (ASPPB) and the National Register of Health Service Providers in Psychology (NR) also developed joint designation criteria that describe an internship (NR, 2004). This criteria, similar in scope and standards to the APPIC membership criteria, assists the NR and the ASPPB staff in defining an internship and determining who is eligible to be listed in the NR (see chap. 11, this volume) or eligible for the ASPPB Certificate of Professional Qualification in Psychology (see chap. 9, this volume).

The American Psychological Association Committee on Accreditation (CoA) has guidelines and procedures (commonly referred to as the G & P) that are used to accredit internship programs (American Psychological Association [APA] Committee on Accreditation, 1997, 2004a). CoA standards provide a very specific framework for internships to follow. Programs must complete an extensive self-study and then representatives of the CoA visit the site. All material is reviewed by the CoA and forms the basis for a decision of the program's accreditation status.

All internship standards are developed to enhance an intern's training experiences. They provide guidance and a framework that can be used by training directors to develop a sequence of procedures that offer a quality training experience.

APPLYING FOR INTERNSHIP

Given the central role that the internship plays in students' graduate training, choosing the right internship program is a high priority for most applicants. Despite the efforts of APPIC to streamline the process of internship application and selection, it remains a time-consuming process.

For many students, preparing for internship begins years before the internship actually commences. We encourage students to seek out a broad range of practicum experiences, with opportunities to work with clients representing a diverse range of backgrounds and presenting issues. These experiences should provide students not only patient contact but also good supervision.

For those students who have an idea about their desired setting or population for internship or after their graduate training, gaining practicum experience in such a setting with such a population is a good idea. Furthermore, students should keep their own comprehensive records (i.e., demographics, setting, services, hours, etc.) of their experiences, as they will be asked to extensively document these experiences during the internship application process. We encourage students to maintain contact with supervisors, faculty, or employers who can write strong letters of recommendation.

LOCATING INTERNSHIP PROGRAMS

In the summer or early fall of the year prior to beginning internship, students should begin the process of searching for internship programs. Most students use the online or printed version of the APPIC Directory, which is the most comprehensive resource available. This directory lists the approximately 600 internship programs that are APPIC members, which includes virtually all APA-accredited programs. The online directory has an extensive set of search options that allow applicants to locate programs of interest. Each program's listing in the APPIC Directory provides information about how to obtain a more extensive description of that program (usually obtained via a link to a Web site).

Applicants are encouraged to seek out programs that are a good fit with their interests, skills, and background, as fit is an important selection criteria for many training directors (Rodolfa et al., 1999). The average applicant applies to approximately 12 to 13 programs (APPIC, 2004b) and the statistics from previous APPIC matches and data gathered from applicants after the match has shown that this is a reasonable number that is manageable for most applicants. Research by APPIC has also demonstrated that applying to more than 15 programs does not increase one's chance of being matched to an internship. However, applying to a small number of programs or all highly competitive programs may reduce the likelihood that an applicant will be successfully placed.

An important consideration in selecting internship programs is their APA–Canadian Psychological Association (CPA) accreditation status and APPIC membership status. APA–CPA accreditation is the highest form of recognition that an internship program can achieve. Typically, experience gained at an accredited internship program will be acceptable to the majority of licensing boards and employers. Although APPIC is not an accrediting body, membership is an indication that the program has been reviewed and meets specific training standards. It is important to understand that there are potential risks to attending a nonaccredited or non-APPIC member program, in that doing so might affect one's ability to get licensed (APA Committee on Accreditation, 2004b) or to work for certain employers (e.g., Veteran's Administration). Students should also check with their doctoral program regarding the minimum criteria (i.e., APA accreditation or APPIC membership) that is acceptable to the program for graduation requirements.

Applicants should also register for the APPIC Match during this period. Complete application materials may be downloaded from the National Matching Services, Inc. (NMS) Web site at http://www.nat match.com.psychint.

The completed application should be submitted directly to NMS along with the appropriate fee. Once NMS receives the application, the applicant will be sent an applicant code number that uniquely identifies him or her in the match.

THE APPLICATION PROCESS

Most internship programs have application deadlines in November, although a few are later. Internship programs generally require the student to submit most or all of the following items as part of their application packet: (a) the APPIC Application for Psychology Internship (AAPI), which is a standardized application form acceptable to almost all programs; (b) a form that verifies that the student is ready for internship, also known as "Part 2" of the AAPI, which is completed by the applicant and his or her director of clinical training; (c) three letters of recommendation (typically two from supervisors and one from a faculty member); (d) a copy of the student's graduate transcripts; and (e) a copy of the applicant's curriculum vita. Although it may or may not be required, it is generally wise to submit a cover letter with these materials as well. Some programs also require the student to submit additional materials, such as a testing report, along with the application. Be sure to carefully follow each program's application instructions as they do vary from site to site.

The AAPI asks the student to summarize relevant background, training, and experience in considerable detail (i.e., client demographics, therapy modalities, tests administered, settings, hours, etc.) as well as respond to several essay questions (e.g., internship goals, biography). Training directors carefully review the AAPI, so it is advisable to get feedback on drafts from trusted faculty and peers. Although completing the AAPI can take a considerable amount of time, it should be noted that its standardized nature means that it can be submitted to virtually all internship programs, thus eliminating the need for each program to require its own separate application.

INTERVIEWS

Once the applicant has submitted his or her application materials, there is generally a 4- to 6-week wait before he or she begins receiving offers for interviews. Each internship program in the APPIC Directory lists the date by which the program has agreed to notify applicants as to whether or not they will receive an interview. Interviews generally occur in January, though some sites may conduct them earlier.

Interviews are typically conducted either on-site or via telephone. Some sites may offer open houses and invite a large number of applicants (sometimes their entire applicant pool) to attend. Even though there is considerable expense in traveling to interviews, many applicants prefer the on-site interview because it generally gives them a better understanding of the internship program. Although it can be challenging to coordinate an interview schedule that minimizes travel time and expenses, most programs will work with the applicant to select interview dates that fit the applicant's schedule.

Applicants should remember that during the interview process they are interviewing sites as well, and should come prepared with questions that will help them better understand the experience and educational aspects of the training program. It is recommended that the applicant carefully review each program's materials prior to the interview, as not being familiar with the program results in a poor impression.

THE APPIC MATCH

APPIC has developed a set of match policies that guide the operation of the process to match applicants and sites. All applicants and programs should be familiar with and abide by these policies. Among other things, the match policies prohibit applicants and sites from discussing ranking information, a restriction that is intended to allow applicants to go through the process without being pressured by programs to reveal or change their rankings.

The match requires each applicant to construct a Rank Order List (ROL). The ROL is simply a list of the programs that the applicant is still considering, sequenced in order of preference. It is extremely important to rank programs in the order in which they are preferred, without taking into account such things as your perception about how likely you will be matched to a particular site, how favorably you think each site is ranking you, and so forth. Although it is natural to contemplate these in your decision-making process, it can result in your getting placed in a less desirable internship program. Simply rank programs in the order in which you want them, and let the computerized matchmaking system do the rest.

Once you have constructed your ROL, you will need to log in to the NMS Web site prior to the deadline date (usually in February) to submit your ROL to the computer. This is a straightforward process that usually only takes a few minutes. If you change your mind about your preferred order of sites, you can always log in again and make the appropriate changes, as long as you do so prior to the deadline.

Once you have submitted your ROL, you must then wait for the match results. As of this writing, APPIC releases the results in two steps generally in late February: (a) on a Friday, when you will receive an e-mail that informs you of whether or not you have been matched to an internship program but not the location of the specific match, and (b) on the following Monday, you will receive another e-mail telling you what location you have been matched with (internship programs are also told on this day the names of the applicants to whom they have been matched). This two-step notification was implemented for the benefit of unmatched applicants, as it provides them "advance notice" on Friday of their unmatched status, allowing them to emotionally and logistically prepare for the opening of the clearinghouse on the following Monday.

It should be noted that the results of the match are binding on all parties: Programs are required to accept the applicants to whom they have been matched and each applicant is required to attend the internship program to which he or she has been matched.

THE APPIC CLEARINGHOUSE

After each match, some applicants do not receive a placement and some programs do not fill all of their positions. The clearinghouse was designed to help applicants learn about positions that remain available after the match. The operation of the clearinghouse can change from year to year. Complete information on the clearinghouse is available at the APPIC Web site at http://www.appic.org.

Problems During Internship

Most interns have a positive internship experience. On occasion, however, an intern may encounter difficulties on-site. If an intern encounters problems with the training staff or program, it is useful to discuss these concerns with the site's director of training. As appropriate, the intern can talk with the other interns or the director of the intern's academic program. Unfortunately, not all problems are easily resolved.

When problems cannot be resolved, APPIC has two programs that may be useful to the interns: Informal Problem Resolution and Formal Complaint Review. With the Informal Problem Resolution, APPIC provides a consultant to help an intern and a site resolve problems that may be encountered. Both interns on-site as well as applicants seeking an internship can use this program. Either sites or interns can contact APPIC to initiate the informal problem resolution process.

If the informal problem resolution process does not provide the needed assistance, APPIC also has a process to review and resolve formal complaints that involve APPIC criteria violations. APPIC will investigate alleged violations of APPIC criteria or policy. If a violation is found, APPIC will determine the appropriate action to resolve the situation. More information about either procedure is available at the APPIC Web site.

In addition to the APPIC procedures, if an intern or training site experiences violations of the APA "Ethical Principles of Psychologists and Code of Conduct" (APA, 2002; see also online version at http://www.apa.org/ethics/), then they can contact the APA Ethics Office. Staff members from the APA Ethics Office will consult with those involved and will also investigate formal complaints.

INTERNSHIP AND LICENSURE

The supervised professional experience accrued during internship is essential to licensing boards. Licensing boards focus on the number of hours successfully accrued as evaluated by the supervisor or training director.

Bartle and Rodolfa (1999) described the relationship between internship hours and the supervised professional experience requirements required by the various states. They compared data from the ASPPB (1997) *Handbook of Licensing and Certification Requirements for Psychologists in the United States and Canada* with data from internship sites. Their study revealed that 11 states required 2,000 hours of supervised professional experience, 14 states required between 1,900 and 1,501 hours, and 14 states required 1,500 hours of supervised experience. In addition, 11 states required 1 year of experience but did not define the number of hours contained in that year of experience.

Almost 75% of the internship sites report that they offer at least 2,000 hours of training. The remaining 25% of sites offer between 1,500 hours to 1,900 hours of supervised professional experience. This data highlights the lack of consistency in licensure requirements across states as well as differences between the number of hours interns receive at training sites.

It is clear that discrepancies in licensing laws exist and variability in the number of hours accrued during internship occurs. Students should be aware of these differences and should know the basic requirements for licensure across states. To help students understand licensing requirements, ASPPB has developed the *Handbook of Licensing and Certification Requirements for Psychologists in the United States and Canada*. It is available online at http://www.asppb.org/handbook/handbook.aspx.

Students and interns will benefit if their training directors help them understand the differences in state laws. Although training directors will not be knowledgeable about all regulations and may not even know the difference between what is a state law and a regulation, they should provide basic information to interns about the process of licensure, the EPPP and other examinations, and the resources about the licensure process.

Conclusion

It is incumbent on students and training directors to tear down the wall that exists between internship and the subsequent sequence of events leading to licensure. Interns can learn about the licensure process by consulting with their training directors, contacting state boards, and using the resources of APPIC, ASPPB, and APA. Training directors are responsible for helping interns learn about the licensure process by initiating discussions, offering seminars, and encouraging ongoing dialogue about licensure. Adequate support from faculty will help interns develop a better understanding of the path to licensure.

References

American Psychological Association. (2002). Ethical principles of psychologists and code of conduct. *American Psychologist, 57,* 1060–1073.

American Psychological Association Committee on Accreditation. (1997). *Book 1: Guidelines and principles for accreditation of programs in professional psychology.* Washington, DC: American Psychological Association.

American Psychological Association Committee on Accreditation. (2004a). *Book 1: Guidelines and principles for accreditation of programs in professional psychology.* Retrieved August 20, 2004, from http://www.apa.org/ed/G&P2.pdf

American Psychological Association Committee on Accreditation. (2004b). *Frequently asked questions about accreditation in psychology.* Retrieved August 20, 2004, from http://www.apa.org/ed/accreditation/accrfaq.html

Association of Psychology Postdoctoral and Internship Centers. (2004a). *APPIC directory 2004–2005* (33rd ed.). Washington, DC: Author.

Association of Psychology Postdoctoral and Internship Centers. (2004b). *APPIC match statistics.* Retrieved August 20, 2004, from http://www.appic.org/match/5_2_2_match_about_statistics.html

Association of Psychology Postdoctoral and Internship Centers. (2004c). *APPIC membership criteria.* Retrieved August 20, 2004, from http://www.APPIC.org

Association of State and Provincial Psychology Boards. (1997). *Handbook of licensing and certification requirements for psychologists in North America*. Montgomery, AL: Author.

Association of State and Provincial Psychology Boards. (2004). *Handbook of licensing and certification requirements for psychologists in the United States and Canada*. Retrieved August 20, 2004, from http://www.asppb.org/handbook/handbook.aspx

Bartle, D., & Rodolfa, E. (1999). Internship hours: Proposing a national standard. *Professional Psychology: Research and Practice, 30,* 420–422.

National Register of Health Service Providers in Psychology. (2004). *ASPPB/National Register designation project*. Retrieved August 20, 2004, from http://www.nationalregister.org/designate.htm

Rodolfa, E. (1999, September). *Internship hours: Truth or dare*. Workshop presented at the Association of Counseling Center Training Agencies National Conference, French Lick, IN.

Rodolfa, E., Vieille, R., Russell, P., Nijjer, S., Nguyen, D., Mendoza, M., & Perrin, L. (1999). Internship selection: Inclusion and exclusion criteria. *Professional Psychology: Research and Practice, 30,* 415–419.

Nadine J. Kaslow and Melanie M. Echols

Postdoctoral Training and Requirements for Licensure and Certification

7

Postdoctoral clinical, counseling, and clinical research experiences have become popular and increasingly necessary for obtaining licensure and employment (Follette & Klesges, 1988; Kaslow, McCarthy, Rogers, & Summerville, 1992; Logsdon-Conradsen et al., 2001; Stewart & Stewart, 1998; Stewart, Stewart, & Vogel, 2000). The number of states requiring postdoctoral training to meet licensure requirements has increased progressively since 1985, when only 20 states required such experiences (Stewart & Stewart, 1998). Myriad professional and personal developmental considerations inform whether or not one chooses to do formalized training versus an informal program of supervised work experience (Kaslow et al., 1992; Logsdon-Conradsen et al., 2001; Stewart et al., 2000). Regardless of the format for the postdoctoral experience, such experiences are most beneficial if they are developmentally informed (Kaslow et al., 1992). This chapter reviews the history of the postdoctoral movement, discusses the role of the Association of Psychology Postdoctoral and Internship Centers (APPIC) in postdoctoral education and training, reviews requirements for postdoctoral training from the American Psychological Association (APA), and discusses the advantages and disadvantages of completing formalized postdoctoral training.

Historical Perspective

At the first national conference to define a training model for professional psychology, the Boulder Conference, the value of postdoctoral training was underscored (Raimy, 1950). The model of education and training articulated at that time called for a 1-year internship in the 3rd year of graduate study. The internship was to be the primary structure for intensive clinical training, after which students would return to the university to complete a clinically informed dissertation. To become proficient in psychotherapy, however, attendees stated that postdoctoral training would be required. Despite proposals at the Stanford (1955) and Miami (1958) conferences for a 4-year academic program followed by a 2-year postdoctoral internship, the 1-year doctoral internship was reaffirmed. At the Chicago Conference, postdoctoral education and training was viewed as a vehicle for the attainment of advanced and specialized skills, and as a means for respecialization. Such training was seen to enhance excellence and be an ethical imperative for people who wanted to teach, supervise, or enter independent practice and practice as an expert (Hoch, Ross, & Winder, 1966). The first conference that focused exclusively on postdoctoral education and training was held at the Menninger Clinic in 1972 (Weiner, 1973). Delegates were concerned about a growing split within the profession between programs focusing on clinical work and those emphasizing research, and underscored the ways in which clinical research was integral to postdoctoral training. No specific guidelines for postdoctoral training were developed.

Throughout the 1980s, guidelines for postdoctoral training in various specialty areas of practice were put forth (e.g., health psychology, clinical child psychology, clinical neuropsychology), but no uniform standards were developed for postdoctoral training in professional psychology. At the Gainesville Conference, the first National Conference on Internship Training in Psychology, it was recommended that internship training be 2 years in length, 1 year predoctoral and 1 year postdoctoral (Belar et al., 1989). However, participants raised concerns about the lack of quality assurance in postdoctoral training and denounced the potential for exploitation of recent graduates (Belar et al., 1989). Delegates highlighted the need for a future conference focused on delineating standards for postdoctoral training that could serve as the basis for accreditation processes. This call occurred simultaneously with the report of the Joint Council on Professional Education in Psychology (JCPEP; Stigall et al., 1990), which also emphasized the need for general standards in postdoctoral training, offered some recommendations, and called for the APA to encourage the development of accredited postdoctoral psychology training programs.

As a follow up to the Gainesville Conference, and in response to the JCPEP report, APPIC sponsored the National Conference on Postdoctoral Training in Professional Psychology (Belar et al., 1993), often referred to as the Ann Arbor Conference. Held in 1992, this conference was cosponsored by APA, the American Board of Professional Psychology (ABPP), the Association of State and Provincial Psychology Boards (ASPPB), and the National Register of Health Service Providers in Psychology (NR). Participants engaged in dialogue about the purpose of postdoctoral training, as well as program models, structures, content, processes, and entrance and exit criteria. Then, the delegates adopted by acclamation a policy statement detailing standards for postdoctoral residency programs, followed by recommendations for a series of initiatives to foster excellence and innovation in training—including a call for accreditation of postdoctoral programs.

In addition to the national conferences, some of the most vocal advocates for accreditation at the postdoctoral level were the specialties in professional psychology. In fact the Midwestern Neuropsychology Consortium of Postdoctoral Fellowship Programs already had developed program self-study procedures and site visit team evaluation forms in accordance with its specialty guidelines. At their encouragement, and to promote a collaborative and cohesive accreditation process for the field, ABPP hosted a meeting at the University of Minnesota in 1991. The outcome of this meeting was the creation of the Interorganizational Council for the Accreditation of Postdoctoral Training Programs. Over the next several years, representatives from the ABPP Board of Trustees and specialty councils, the NR, ASPPB, APPIC, and APA delineated the most appropriate mechanisms for the field to accredit postdoctoral programs. By 1995, the IOC in coordination with the APA's Committee on Accreditation (CoA) developed generic guidelines and procedures building on the recommendations of the Ann Arbor Conference and the CoA's newly developed guidelines for accreditation at the doctoral level. In 1996, the CoA and the APA Council of Representatives formally adopted guidelines for the accreditation of postdoctoral education and training programs in professional psychology. In 1997, the first postdoctoral programs were accredited.

As of 2005, 39 states require 1 year of postdoctoral supervised work experience prior to licensure; 8 states and the District of Columbia require 2 years of postdoctoral supervised work experience prior to licensure; and 2 states do not have a postdoctoral supervised work experience requirement (see http://www.asppb.org/). The number of states requiring postdoctoral training to meet licensure requirements has increased progressively since 1985, when only 29 states required postdoctoral training experience (Stewart & Stewart, 1998). States vary on required total postdoctoral hours, which average between 1,000 and 2,000 hours for states requiring at least 1 year of postdoctoral training, and between 1,500 and 4,000 hours for states requiring 2 years of postdoctoral training. States also vary on the number of direct client–patient contact hours needed to complete licensure requirements. On average, most states require between 450 and 1,000 client contact hours. Consistent weekly supervision is required by all of the states for licensure.

Over the years there has been growing controversy regarding the need for the supervised postdoctoral work experience prior to licensure. Proponents of maintaining this requirement, as well as advocates for eliminating this requirement, have articulated their views at multiple forums, including the Commission on Education and Training Leading to Licensure (APA, 2001). Rather than making a final determination at this meeting regarding this requirement, there was a decision to examine the competencies expected of licensed professional psychologists and then to ascertain when in the education and training sequence such competencies were attained. These issues were addressed to some extent at the Competencies Conference: Future Directions in Education and Credentialing in Professional Psychology (Kaslow, 2004; Kaslow et al., 2004).

There has been a demand from many students and new professionals to eliminate the postdoctoral requirement. The argument to eliminate the additional training centers on the issues of heavy debt from student loans, problems finding suitable postdoctoral positions with adequate supervision and compensation, and the length of training commitments in comparison to other healthcare disciplines. In the view of many students and professionals, training programs provide students with extensive clinical experiences obtained through practicums, predoctoral internships, and other work experiences (France & Wolf, 2000), leading some to argue that the addition of a postdoctoral requirement is viewed as unnecessary. One study in which predoctoral interns were surveyed found that a significant percentage of interns (e.g., 22%) did not believe that they needed additional training to achieve their career goals (Stewart et al., 2000). However, despite the additional training obligations, most interns believe that they could benefit from additional supervised experience to hone their skills and consolidate their identities as professionals (Stewart et al., 2000). In addition, many people affiliated with professional psychology support the requirements of a supervised postdoctoral experience before licensure and assert that this additional experience benefits new graduates, the entire field of psychology, and the consumers of psychological services (Belar, 1992;

DeFrancesco, 1992; France & Wolf, 2000; Graham & Fox, 1991; Toye & Pierce, 1987; Tuma, 1989).

APPIC CRITERIA FOR POSTDOCTORAL RESIDENCY PROGRAMS

In 1991, in response to the growing number of states requiring postdoctoral training for licensure and the awareness that additional required supervised training after the attainment of the doctoral degree is important, the Association of Psychology Internship Centers became APPIC and delineated criteria for postdoctoral training programs to be listed in the *APPIC Directory*. The current APPIC membership criteria for postdoctoral training programs are as follows: (a) an organized experience with a planned programmed sequence of supervised training experiences; (b) a designated licensed psychologist who is responsible for the integrity and quality of the training program, with expertise in the area of postdoctoral training, active research productivity, and evidence of professional competence and leadership; (c) two or more licensed psychologists on staff and a training faculty with at least one psychologist with expertise in each area of postdoctoral training offered; (d) a minimum of 2 hours per week of regularly scheduled, face-to-face, individual supervision with a licensed psychologist associated with the program with the specific intent of dealing with psychological services rendered directly by the fellow; (e) at least 2 additional hours of learning activities, clinical seminars, cotherapy with a staff person, group supervision, and additional supervision; and (f) the assurance that 25% of the postdoctoral fellow's time is engaged in professional psychological services. Postdoctoral fellows are required to have completed all professional doctoral degree requirements from an APA–Canadian Psychological Association accredited program and a predoctoral internship that meets APPIC standards.

The training program at the sponsoring institution is required to have at least one fellow on-site and in training at the time of their initial application for APPIC membership. Also, the institution must have written statements or brochures available to describe the goals and the content of the program, the program's organization, the entrance requirements, the faculty and staff, and the program's mechanisms for fellow evaluation. These institutions should also have documented due process procedures, which are given to the fellows at the beginning of the training period. The postdoctoral training program requires a minimum of 1,500 hours that must be completed in no less than 9 months and no more than 24 months (2 years half-time); however, depending on the area of specialty practice, the program may be more than 1 year. At the conclusion of the fellowship and fulfillment of the program requirements, a certificate of completion is granted to the fellow.

According to the *2003–2004 APPIC Directory*, there were 77 APPIC member programs, and this included all of the APA-accredited programs. There were a total of 307 full-time slots and the mean salary was $31,400. Typically, programs seek APPIC membership first and then go on to obtain APA accreditation.

In addition to ascertaining if programs provide appropriate training and to offering a list of postdoctoral training sites through the directory, APPIC offers other services to postdoctoral trainers and fellows. For example, on APPIC's Web site there are a host of training resources, and APPIC sponsors an electronic mailing list for postdoctoral fellows and those applying for programs. APPIC also offers an informal problem resolution program that helps fellows and sites deal with challenging situations. They offer guidance on a broad array of topics, such as issues related to the Family and Medical Leave Act. They advocate for postdoctoral issues at the national level in terms of federal funding, issues related to supply and demand, and the appropriate types and levels of competence for various credentials.

APA ACCREDITATION OF POSTDOCTORAL RESIDENCIES

Although postdoctoral training has a long history in professional psychology, there was no formal accreditation of postdoctoral programs until 1997, when the APA CoA approved two postdoctoral residencies, one at the Harbor-UCLA Medical Center and one at the Menninger Clinic. As of June 2004, there were 20 accredited programs in professional psychology (i.e., substantive areas of clinical, counseling, and school psychology), three in clinical health psychology, six in clinical neuropsychology, and one in rehabilitation psychology, for a total of 30 programs. Consistent with the roots of doctoral accreditation, the Veteran's Administration is playing a significant role in the growing number of accredited programs ($n = 13$). In addition, there are 11 accredited programs in medical schools, three in federal agencies (e.g., military), and three are consortium-based.

The accreditation process for postdoctoral residencies is consistent with that of the doctoral and internship levels in that it involves a professional judgment as to the degree to which a program has achieved the goals and objectives of its stated training model. A core principle is as follows:

> Postdoctoral residency education and training in professional psychology reflect the natural evolution and expansion of the

knowledge base of the science and practice of psychology, and should be of sufficient breadth to ensure advanced competence as a professional psychologist and of sufficient depth and focus to ensure technical expertise and proficiency in the substantive traditional or specialty practice areas of professional psychology for which the residents are being prepared. (APA, 2000, p. 3)

To become accredited, a program must publicly state a goal of preparation for advanced practice in a substantive traditional or specialty practice area. In addition to specifying the advanced competencies that residents are to achieve in assessment, intervention, consultation, program evaluation, supervision, teaching, administration, and professional conduct, advanced competencies in strategies of scholarly inquiry must also be articulated. The criteria related to program length specifies a minimum of 1 year, although it is acknowledged that up to 3 years may be required for some specialty areas of practice. To help with the review of specialized postdoctoral programs, the CoA augmented the general guidelines with specialty-specific guidelines received from organizations that have membership on the Council of Specialties.

Formal Versus Informal Postdoctoral Training

Both formalized postdoctoral residencies and postdoctoral supervised work experiences can satisfy state licensure requirements. However, formalized postdoctoral fellowships are organized programs designed to provide advanced or specialized training, whereas a supervised work experience typically is crafted to satisfy licensure requirements. Formalized training programs typically are a minimum of 1 year full time or 2 years half time and usually include some combination of direct service activities along with training and didactic activities. Many of these programs offer some research component as well. Supervised work experience in regular employment settings commonly entails more direct service hours and may be associated with more professional autonomy. When such work experiences are gained in institutional settings, the positions typically come with higher salaries. However, when such experiences are obtained in private practice settings, the salaries are much more variable and there may be less access to benefit programs.

A survey of predoctoral interns revealed that approximately 25% of them desired formalized, programmatic postdoctoral training

Most of the state, provincial, and territorial boards now have Web sites with information on standards and the application process. For specific information on the various licensure and certification requirements in the United States and Canada, go to http://www.asppb.org/ or http://www.nationalregister.org/links_licensingboards.htm and hyperlink to the licensing board Web site of the jurisdiction in which you intend to seek licensure.

CRITERION 4: ADHERENCE TO PROFESSIONAL ETHICS

The fourth criterion is that the applicant must attest to whether or not there are any disciplinary actions against the license currently held or any previous license. Assuming no disciplinary history, which is checked against the NR disciplinary database and the ASPPB data bank, the application is forwarded for final review. If, however, the applicant has a disciplinary history, then primary source documentation from the disciplining body is obtained and the applicant has the opportunity to provide his or her perspective on the basis for the sanction and any remediation that has occurred. This information is forwarded to the Committee on Professional Practice and Ethics for consideration under the guidelines developed by the NR (n.d.c).

Once the doctoral degree in psychology, 2 years of supervised experience in health service provision including an internship and 1 year of postdoctoral experience, a license to practice psychology, and the absence of professional ethics and conduct have been demonstrated satisfactorily, you can become credentialed as a health service provider in psychology.

When to Apply for the National Register Credential

There are two choices you have with regard to applying for the NR credential. One option is to apply at the time that you have fully completed all the requirements (internship, doctoral degree, supervised postdoctoral experience, and unrestricted psychology license). If you apply at the same time that you apply for a license, it may be easier in that you are requesting the documentation at the same time. Also, applying for the NR at that time allows you to take advantage of reduced NR renewal fees for 3 years following your first license.

However, doctoral students do not need to wait until they are licensed before they can apply to the NR. The National Psychologist Trainee Register (NPTR) was initiated in 1998 to facilitate the psychology graduate students' early access to the sequence of licensing and credentialing steps. Through participation in the NPTR program, graduate students document each phase of their education and training in a sequential fashion, having each part reviewed at the time of completion to determine compliance with national standards. Signing up for the NPTR is free to any doctoral student and can be quickly completed online. Registering early in your training provides access to helpful information, resources, and publications. Graduate students who apply through the NPTR will have more rapid access to the NR credential as soon as they are independently licensed. In the interim, the names and approved credentials of graduate students are listed on the NPTR online database. Publications and industry news are sent by the NR to NPTR participants free of charge (see NR, n.d.i).

WHY SHOULD GRADUATE STUDENTS APPLY FOR THE NATIONAL REGISTER THROUGH THE NATIONAL PSYCHOLOGIST TRAINEE REGISTER?

The most obvious reason to apply through the NPTR is to position yourself for obtaining the NR credential, and the benefits that come with the distinction including licensure mobility, visibility, credentials verification to health care panels, free continuing education, and publications. In addition, it is considerably easier, and less expensive, to apply for the NR credential through the NPTR. One of the most frequent problems that regular applicants for the NR encounter is unavailability of supervisors, training directors, or program directors. The NPTR can assist you in developing and maintaining a credentials profile that complies with national standards at a time when the psychologists who trained and supervised you are still available to document your completion of program requirements and adherence to the standards.

To position yourself for success in your professional life, you need to learn about credentialing and certification issues as early as possible. Some doctoral programs include a professional issues course that covers credentialing and certification issues, but not all do, and the quality and thoroughness of professional issue classes vary. Therefore, the best way for students to learn about credentialing and certification is to get involved with the largest credentialing organization for psychologists by applying through the NPTR.

THE NATIONAL REGISTER AND CANADIAN REGISTER EXPEDITE LICENSURE MOBILITY

Students often refer to licensure mobility as an important credentialing benefit. In the United States, the National Register is approved in numerous jurisdictions to expedite licensure mobility for Registrants by endorsing credentials to licensing boards, often eliminating the need for Registrants to provide transcripts, internship and postdoctoral confirmation forms, and national exam scores when applying for licensure. The NR has also been approved to expedite licensure by endorsement in most Canadian jurisdictions (North–South mobility) for those applicants currently licensed in the United States. In Canada, the NR and the Canadian Register are both recognized in all provinces to expedite mobility by endorsement for psychologists currently licensed in one province and applying for licensure in another province (East–West mobility).

An important distinction for students is that the NR and Canadian Register do not require applicants to be licensed for 5 years before they may take advantage of expedited mobility, as is the case with the Certificate of Professional Qualification (see NR, n.d.h, for more information).

THE NATIONAL REGISTER EDUCATIONAL REQUIREMENTS: A RESOURCE FOR STUDENTS

Regardless of whether a graduate student in psychology applies through the NPTR or not, the NR offers a valuable resource to students currently in training and those considering pursuing a doctoral degree in psychology. To assist licensing and credentialing organizations as well as students in recognizing which programs meet national standards, the NR created the Designation Project in 1980. The ASPPB joined the Designation Project in 1986. The ASPPB/NR Designation Project reviews applicant doctoral programs that are training students for professional practice to determine if their publicly available documentation demonstrates that the programs meet the designation criteria (see NR, n.d.d for the guidelines). The list of approved doctoral programs helps students to determine in advance whether a potential doctoral psychology program will meet the standards for licensure and for credentialing. Also, as most licensing bodies have adopted these criteria in whole or in part, the list also aids licensure boards in determining whether the licensure applicant has completed a program that should meet their own licensure requirements.

An important distinction among the designation and the accreditation process is that doctoral programs in any area of psychology may apply for designation, not just in clinical, counseling, or school psychology areas. Once approved, the program is added to the online list of designated programs (NR, n.d.b). This online resource greatly facilitates the review of applicants for licensure. Students who are considering enrollment in a doctoral program to pursue a professional practice in psychology should first contact the jurisdiction in which they intend to seek licensure to determine the exact education and training requirements for licensure. If the licensing board recommends or requires that the doctoral program be APA accredited, CPA accredited, or ASPPB/ National Register designated, then students can then access the online listing of designated programs to determine whether their program of interest meets these requirements (refer to http://www.national register.org/designate_stsearch.html).

A Historical Perspective: The Canadian Register

In 1985, the Council of Provincial Associations of Psychologists and its member bodies established the Canadian Register of Health Service Providers in Psychology. The Canadian Register was created in response to an increased need to identify psychologists who met the basic criteria for the provision of health services in Canada. It was established in 1985 on receipt of its letters patent and articles of incorporation from the federal Ministry of Consumer and Corporate Affairs. The associations and regulatory bodies of Alberta, British Columbia, Manitoba, New Brunswick, Newfoundland, Northwest Territories, Nova Scotia, Ontario, Prince Edward Island, Quebec, and Saskatchewan, as well as by the Canadian Psychological Association, ratified the constitution and are the member bodies of the Canadian Register. The NR served as an important model for the implementation of the Canadian Register and the organizations have maintained a close liaison relationship since 1985.

The Mission of the Canadian Register

To realize its mission, the Canadian Register offers the following services:

- advocates recognition of health service psychologists in primary care reform and health care reform;
- supports the marketing and promotion of health service psychologists in the business sector;
- enables registrants to more adequately meet increased demands for accountability through providing continuing education; and
- establishes interorganizational collaboration, such as promoting mobility mechanisms within Canada and across national borders. (Canadian Register of Health Service Providers in Psychology, 1999)

The Canadian Register contributed to the mutual recognition agreement signed by all Canadian regulatory bodies of psychology in 2001 and assists in its implementation. For the past 10 years it also worked closely with the NR and other national organizations from Canada, Mexico, and the United States by participating in the Trilateral Forum on Professional Psychology.

Eligibility Criteria for the Canadian Register Credential

For the most part, the purposes of the Canadian Register are similar to that of the National Register, but there are differences in their eligibility criteria and review process. For the Canadian Register, graduate degrees are vetted by the provincial or territorial regulatory bodies of psychology. This reflects both the corporate member standing of the Canadian regulatory bodies in the Canadian Register's organizational structure as well as their commitment to support the regulatory bodies' decisions. Another significant difference is that it is also still possible for a psychologist with a master's degree to be eligible for the Canadian Register, which is still in its grandparent period.

The Canadian Register has maintained both a normative route as well as alternative mechanisms to admission, as the grandparent provisions initiated in 1985 and due to expire in 2000 were extended through the end of 2010. Basically, the options include one similar to the NR (doctoral degree plus 2 years of supervised health service provision experience), another that allows under certain circumstances for a doctoral degree plus 4 years of experience to qualify, and others involving several routes based on a master's degree plus 2 to 6 years of experience. Please go to http://www.crhspp.ca/ for the detailed provisions (Canadian Register of Health Service Providers in Psychology, 1999).

Conclusion

Improving the identification of and access to qualified health service providers in psychology for both the private and public sectors has been at the forefront of strategic priorities for professional psychology in the United States and Canada for several decades. The NR and Canadian Register credentials were created to support these goals. Professional psychology requires a credible national credential to assist the general public as well as private and public sector decision makers to identify qualified health service providers. Even though the health care system in the United States is primarily privately funded and Canadian health care is primarily publicly funded, the NR and the Canadian Register are both committed to supporting their registrants through a variety of initiatives such as continuing education and practice enhancement activities that evolve to meet emerging societal needs. This commitment has ensured that both organizations serve the profession and the public admirably.

References

American Psychological Association. (2004). *Accredited doctoral programs in professional psychology.* Retrieved February 7, 2006, from http://www.apa.org/ed/accreditation/doctoral.html

Canadian Psychological Association. (n.d.). *CPA accredited programs.* Retrieved February 7, 2006, from http://www.cpa.ca/cpasite/showPage.asp?id=10042&fr=

Canadian Register of Health Service Providers in Psychology. (1999). *About the Canadian register.* Retrieved February 7, 2006, from http://www.crhspp.ca/aboutus.htm

National Register of Health Service Providers in Psychology. (n.d.a). *Designated doctoral programs in psychology.* Retrieved February 7, 2006, from http://www.nationalregister.org/designate.htm

National Register of Health Service Providers in Psychology. (n.d.b). *Doctoral psychology programs meeting designation criteria.* Retrieved February 7, 2006, from http://www.nationalregister.org/designate_stsearch.html

National Register of Health Service Providers in Psychology. (n.d.c). *For the public: Guidelines concerning removal from listing related to professional conduct.* Retrieved February 7, 2006, from http://www. nationalregister.org/withdrawalguidelines.htm

National Register of Health Service Providers in Psychology. (n.d.d). *Guidelines for defining a doctoral degree in psychology.* Retrieved February 7, 2006, from http://www.nationalregister.org/doctoraldegrees. html

National Register of Health Service Providers in Psychology. (n.d.e). *Guidelines for defining an internship or organized health service training program in psychology.* Retrieved February 7, 2006, from http:// www.nationalregister.org/internshipguidelines.html

National Register of Health Service Providers in Psychology. (n.d.f). *Guidelines for supervised postdoctoral experience.* Retrieved February 7, 2006, from http://www.nationalregister.org/postdoc.html

National Register of Health Service Providers in Psychology. (n.d.g). *How to read online listings in national psychologist trainee register* (Bullet 8). Retrieved February 7, 2006, from http://www.national register.org/nptr_glossaryofterms.htm

National Register of Health Service Providers in Psychology. (n.d.h). *Mobility for registrants.* Retrieved February 7, 2006, from http:// www.nationalregister.org/mobility.htm

National Register of Health Service Providers in Psychology. (n.d.i). *National psychologist trainee register application request form.* Retrieved February 7, 2006, from http://www.nationalregister.org/nptrapp. htm

National Register of Health Service Providers in Psychology. (n.d.j). *National Register mission statement.* Retrieved February 7, 2006, from http://www.nationalregister.org/aboutus_mission.htm

Patricia M. Bricklin and Janet Ciuccio

Creating Certification and Examination Programs: The College of Professional Psychology

12

F rom the perspective of a graduate student, achieving the doctorate in psychology and becoming licensed as a psychologist are formidable goals. However, beyond basic licensing as a psychologist, there are a number of additional credentials that can be earned by a developing psychologist (e.g., achieving health service provider status, specialty diplomates and certificates of knowledge, and skills in such focused areas as alcohol and other psychoactive substance abuse). The College of Professional Psychology is one such certifying entity. These credentials are voluntary, for the most part, but serve important functions both for the psychologist and the consuming public.

This chapter introduces the College's purpose and the various functions it may serve in the professional development of psychologists. The requirements and the process of attainment of such certifications are also reviewed.

The College of Professional Psychology

To understand the function of the College today and how it may have an impact on students' future practice, it is necessary to briefly describe the changing face of psychological practice that began around the early 1990s. Just prior to 1991, the environment of psychological practice began to change. Psychologists in practice began to find themselves increasingly challenged by a marketplace that was becoming more demanding of credible evidence of a practitioner's ability to provide specified services. An increasing number of members of other professions competed for these positions. Managed care entities, consumer groups, and other payers of mental health services frequently found themselves in the position of looking for health professionals who could evidence proof of expertise in a particular area. Because of the generic nature of the psychology licensing laws and the broad array of knowledge and skills within psychological practice, it was difficult for them to identify individual practitioners with the specific skills being sought. As a result, the value of psychologists' expertise was often overlooked or at least misunderstood. In response to these threats, in 1994 the American Psychological Association (APA) Council of Representatives created the College of Professional Psychology (APA Council of Representatives, 1994).

The College is the entity housed currently within the APA Practice Organization that develops and implements certification programs in areas of psychology that are not specialties but do require special knowledge and skills and for which there is a demonstrated public need for a special credential. As of 2005, the College issues certificates in one area, Alcohol and Other Psychoactive Substance Abuse Disorders, to those licensed psychologists who apply, meet the qualifications, and successfully pass the exam in that area.

To date, the College has reviewed a number of substantive areas for possible certification (e.g., geropsychology, biofeedback, and executive coaching). The development of a certification program in any area that includes a valid examination is an expensive process. A real need for a cost-effective certificate in an area must be demonstrated before the College can proceed to develop a new certification program. No other areas have been authorized by the APA Council of Representatives.

THE ALCOHOL AND OTHER PSYCHOACTIVE SUBSTANCE ABUSE CERTIFICATE

In August 2004, the Council of Representatives also recognized the treatment of alcohol and other psychoactive substance use disorders as a practice proficiency and authorized the College to develop a certification in this treatment area (APA Council of Representatives, 1994). A computer-administered examination became available in June 1996, and is administered nationwide. Reports from candidates who have taken the examination indicate that the exam has an appropriate breadth of coverage, and that questions are clearly worded and are related to practice.

The Certificate of Proficiency is offered to psychologists who meet the following criteria:

- have a current state or provincial license in good standing to engage in the independent practice of psychology;
- provide health services in psychology;
- have been engaged, as licensed psychologists, in the treatment of alcohol and other psychoactive substance use disorders for at least 1 year during the last 3 years; and
- successfully complete the certification examination developed by the College of Professional Psychology for the treatment of alcohol and other psychoactive substance use disorders. (College of Professional Psychology, APA Practice Organization, 2001a)

The Certificate of Proficiency is offered to all licensed health service provider psychologists who meet these eligibility criteria, regardless of APA membership status. Candidates for examination receive a detailed explanation of the knowledge domain in addition to a list of suggested readings for review of critical information. These can be obtained from the College of Professional Psychology, APA Practice Organization, 750 First Street NE, Washington, DC 20002.

The knowledge domain covers clinical pharmacology and clinical epidemiology of psychoactive substances; etiology of psychoactive substance use disorders; initiation, progression, and maintenance of psychoactive substance use disorders; course and natural history of psychoactive substance use disorders, prevention, early intervention, and harm reduction; screening and assessment of psychoactive substance use; diagnosis and comorbidity; Treatment I: models and approaches; Treatment II: planning, implementing, and managing treatment and the course of recovery; issues in specific populations; research knowledge; and legal and ethical issues (College of Professional Psychology, APA Practice Organization, 2001a).

Since receipt of its first application in early 1996, the College has received approximately 2,800 applications for certification. Of those 2,800, approximately 2,500 psychologists became certified. A measure of progress in terms of the utility of the certification is the fact that it is currently recognized by seven states, each in slightly different ways, but all in ways that permit psychologists to expand their opportunities to provide services in this treatment area. State agencies in Georgia, Hawaii, Indiana, New Hampshire, North Carolina, Vermont, and Wisconsin cite the certification. In addition, hospitals, payers, and provider panels have recognized the certification as potential evidence of training and competence. Psychologists who have earned and maintained their certificate have found it useful and sometimes necessary in their practices.

THE PSYCHOPHARMACOLOGY EXAM FOR PSYCHOLOGISTS

The idea of developing an examination in psychopharmacology that would meet potential credentialing standards and measure credibly the knowledge base of competence necessary to prescribe developed from discussions among the members of the APA Committee for the Advancement of Professional Practice, the APA College of Professional Psychology, and Russ Newman, Executive Director of the APA Practice Directorate. It was believed that such an exam would advance the prescriptive authority agenda, which is a priority for APA. A valid and legally defensible, secure exam would give reassurance to states or provincial licensing boards that those with the necessary education and training who took and passed the exam would be qualified (see chap.14, this volume).

In August 1997, the APA Council of Representatives authorized the development of the Psychology Examination in Psychopharmacology (PEP) by the College of Professional Psychology for use by state and provincial licensing authorities (should they choose to use it) in granting prescriptive authority to psychologists (APA Council of Representatives, 1997). The College appointed a multidisciplinary panel and chose the Professional Examination Service (PES) of New York to guide the exam development.

Since 1999, the College has administered and banked the scores of candidates with approved qualifications who took the exam. This aggregated data (when large enough) may be useful to psychopharmacology education programs, the practice community, and those working in the advocacy arena. An individual score will be released to a state board when requested by an examinee.

Minimum requirements to be admitted to take the PEP examination include the following criteria:

- doctoral degree in psychology;
- provision of health services in psychology;
- current psychology license in good standing to engage in the independent practice of psychology; and
- successful completion of a postdoctoral program of education in an organized program of intensive didactic instruction. (College of Professional Psychology, APA Practice Organization Brochure, 2001b)

The knowledge-based content areas assessed by the PEP are integrating clinical psychopharmacology with the practice of psychology, neuroscience, nervous system pathology, physiology and pathophysiology, biopsychosocial and pharmacologic assessment and monitoring, differential diagnosis, pharmacology, clinical psychopharmacology, research, and professional, legal, and interprofessional issues. Examinees receive a report of their overall performance on the exam as well as their performance on the knowledge-based content areas of the exam.

As of August 2004, New Mexico and Louisiana passed prescribing laws for psychologists and have developed regulations to implement these laws. As with any change-making endeavor, these laws were not achieved easily. However, the PEP, as articulated by the College in 1997, is increasingly being used by these licensing boards and may fulfill the prediction that the availability of a valid, legally defensible, exam can shorten the time between the implementation of laws and the availability of psychologists to prescribe.

Conclusion

At the present time, your interest and need for services from the College may only be the certification in alcohol and other psychoactive substance abuse disorders or taking and passing the Psychopharmacology Exam for Psychologists, as a prerequisite to medical consultation or in some states, prescribing. As areas of practice for psychologists expand and newly emerging areas evolve, additional certification or some other methods of demonstrating knowledge and skills may be needed. In response to a future need the College may expand its certification programs and develop other functions. What might those be? Can you see yourself seeking certifications in special areas and playing a role in future change-making endeavors? Remember that this future will depend on both the emerging developments in the field and the vision of present and future psychologists like you.

References

American Psychological Association Council of Representatives. (1994, August). *Minutes from meeting Creating College of Professional Psychology*. Washington, DC: Author.

American Psychological Association Council of Representatives. (1997, August). *Minutes from meeting Authorizing Development of Psychopharmacology Exam.* Washington, DC: Author.

College of Professional Psychology, APA Practice Organization. (2001a). *Certificate of proficiency in the treatment of alcohol and other substance use disorders* [Brochure]. Washington, DC: American Psychological Association.

College of Professional Psychology, APA Practice Organization. (2001b). *Psychopharmacology examination for psychologists* [Brochure]. Washington, DC: American Psychological Association.

Judith S. Blanton

License Issues for Industrial/ Organizational Psychologists and Other Non-Health Service Providers

13

Many people, including many psychologists, incorrectly assume that only clinical, counseling, and school psychologists must be licensed. It is true that exceptions to licensure are typically given to those who work in governmental agencies or universities. Yet only a handful of jurisdictions exempt industrial/organizational (I/O) psychologists or others who do not provide direct mental health or health services (*non-health service providers* or *non-HSPs*). In the majority of jurisdictions, licensure is required if the psychologist does work "of a psychological nature" and the jurisdictional "scope of practice" typically involves work that would be done by I/O or consultants, not only work done by therapists. University professors who are exempted as academics but who have private consulting practices may well be required to hold a license for their consulting work. Laws and regulations vary a great deal from state to state (or province to province in Canada). North Dakota and Tennessee, for example, even specify that psychological licensure is required "regardless of whether payment is received for services rendered" (Tennessee Board of Examiners in Psychology, 2005).

Because of the great variability and complexity of licensure laws, there is much confusion and misinformation about licensure laws and regulations, particularly those for non-HSPs. The purpose of this chapter is twofold. First, it is designed to assist students and their faculty advisors in determining if licensure is necessary and, if so, to identify the steps needed to become licensed. Second, it is designed to raise awareness about the special challenges faced by those that are now termed non-HSPs. It is hoped that awareness of these issues will influence boards of psychology and legislators to develop laws and regulations that are more appropriate for I/O psychologists, consultants, and other non-HSPs. The bottom line is that in most jurisdictions, I/O psychologists and consulting psychologists are required to be licensed to practice.

It is important to begin with a caveat. There is enormous variability among states in their licensure laws and regulations. It is therefore critical that students read the regulations for the specific jurisdiction in which they plan to practice. The format of these documents is often written in legal jargon and may be ambiguous. It may also be useful to contact the licensing board directly. When doing so, make sure that you speak to someone who is highly knowledgeable because entry level staff may be unfamiliar with exemptions or special options that may be available for those who are not planning to practice in the clinical, counseling, or school area. The Association of State and Provincial Psychology Boards (ASPPB, 2002) has a document available on its Web site that provides short summaries of the laws and regulations of each state or province (see http://www.asppb.org). The Society for Industrial and Organizational Psychology has a "tool kit" for students that provides useful information about licensure. There is also a link to the jurisdictional Web sites that provide information about each state or province (see http://www.siop.org).

Why Be Licensed?

It may be useful to begin with asking the question, Why be licensed as an I/O psychologist or other non-HSP? There are at least four reasons, which are explained here.

1. Because it is the law in most jurisdictions.

   Today, most jurisdictions have "generic" licensing laws which require anyone practicing psychology to be licensed. Licenses typically look and read the same whether the person is a clinical, organizational, consulting, or counseling psychologist. About a dozen jurisdictions, in one way or another, exempt I/O psychologists (in most cases with the stipulation that they do not provide "direct services" to individual clients). A few jurisdictions specifically limit licensing to health service or psychotherapy providers (e.g., Colorado) but, again, the general rule is that a psychologist must be licensed to practice psychology. Most jurisdictions define the scope of the practice of psychology broadly. Some specifically mention areas that are related to consulting or I/O work. For example, the scope of practice for Maine includes "psychological consulting to individuals and organizations" (Office of Licensing and Registration, 2004). New York specifically includes "personnel selection and management; the arrangement of effective work and learning situations, advertising and market research, the resolution of interpersonal and social conflicts, lecturing on or teaching of psychology and the design and conduct of applied psychological research" (New York State Education Department, Office of the Professions, 2004).

Historically, a few jurisdictions did not have "practice laws" but instead had "title laws" that regulated the use of the title "psychologist" (see chap. 2, this volume). Thus, some I/O and other non-HSPs who did not want to be licensed could call themselves something else, such as management consultant, to avoid licensure. The current move away from title laws and toward practice laws makes this option less viable. Although I/O practitioners, to date, have seldom been called to task by boards for doing this, if a complaint were filed, they could face serious legal prosecution. They could also face ethical charges from the American Psychological Association (APA) if they were found to be working within the scope of practice defined by their jurisdiction without a license. This could be financially and professionally disastrous.

2. Being licensed increases credibility.

Having gone through the licensing process is an indication of competence and documents the quality of training and supervision as well as the level of fitness for practice. Some years ago, a well-known ex-APA president was asked to testify in court. When he was asked for his license number, he indicated that he was not licensed. In that state, academics were exempt from licensure, but this did not matter to the judge and he dismissed the psychologist without allowing him to testify (he then got licensed). Licensing is also an indication by the jurisdiction that you are a "real" psychologist. One's identity as a psychologist is related to this endorsement by the governmental institution.

3. Being licensed protects you.

　　If licensed, you have access to liability insurance that a non-licensed person does not have. If challenged legally, you can cite your license as an indicator of your expertise.

4. Being licensed provides your clients with the ability to claim privilege and thus allows you to promise confidentiality.

　　If you are licensed, then it is unethical and illegal for you to share confidential information about that client without permission from the client. If you are not licensed, your clients have no legal claim to psychological privilege. Although a nonlicensed person can promise confidentiality, he or she has no legal basis for this. Obviously, a licensed person can be subpoenaed and forced to testify, but having the license makes this less likely and more difficult. Without a license, your records are just as accessible as a beautician's or an architect's. When clients ask me if I will keep things confidential, I can say that if I fail to do so, I will lose my license. This can be reassuring to clients.

WHAT ARE THE REQUIREMENTS FOR INDUSTRIAL/ORGANIZATIONAL PSYCHOLOGISTS AND OTHER NON-HEALTH SERVICE PROVIDERS?

There are general requirements for the licensure of all psychologists. These requirements involve academic standards, hours of supervised work, written and sometimes oral examinations, and special or continuing education courses. Although a number of groups are working to modify some of these requirements, as they currently stand some of these pose problems for non-HSP psychologists. Many of the laws and regulations were designed with clinicians in mind and therefore do not fit the realities of non-HSP training and practice. Each issue is discussed subsequently and efforts to make licensure more realistic for consulting and I/O psychologists are outlined.

ACADEMIC PROGRAMS

In general, having graduated from a regionally accredited program that is clearly "psychological in nature" is sufficient. However, at least a dozen jurisdictions, including Kansas, Nebraska, and Montana, require the doctoral degree to be from an APA accredited (or equivalent) program. Because APA only accredits clinical, counseling, and school programs, psychologists from other programs face an additional need to document their training. You may be asked to provide transcripts or other documentation about your curriculum to prove equivalency. Doctoral programs that are recognized by the Joint ASPPB/National Register (NR) Designation are often automatically approved as meeting academic requirements (National Register of Health Service Providers in Psychology, 2005). A number of I/O programs are a part of this registry. A list of doctoral programs meeting ASPPB/NR Designation Criteria can be found at http://www.nationalregister.org/designate_stsearch.html. Check with a faculty member or program administrator to determine if this registry recognizes your program and, if it does not, then encourage your program administration to explore obtaining this. Also check with your specific state's regulations to determine whether they require specific coursework (e.g., "biological bases of behavior," a course that some I/O schools do not have). If specific courses are required, then it is better to take them prior to graduation (see chap. 1, this volume). Some states allow a few postdoctoral courses to be taken to meet the academic requirements but, again, this varies. Furthermore, it is frustrating and logistically complex for someone who has already graduated to take additional courses merely to meet specific requirements and this process can delay one's ability to obtain licensure by many months.

SUPERVISION

In general, jurisdictions require approximately 3,000 to 4,000 hours of supervised experience to become licensed as a psychologist. The general hours do not pose major difficulties; however, the specifics regarding when and how these hours are to be accrued may. Typically one is allowed to do half of those hours in a predoctoral internship, but it is also possible to do all of the hours at the postdoctoral level. Again, jurisdictions differ. A number of states (e.g., Washington, Tennessee, and New Hampshire) now require a predoctoral internship that is APA-accredited. There is no APA accreditation of I/O internships. This is a problem for non-HSPs, yet efforts to improve the supervision regulations are being made. The ASPPB, an organization comprising all the U.S. and Canadian psychology boards, has issued a report that addresses supervision of I/O psychologists (ASPPB, 2003). The following is an excerpt from that document:

> There are two major challenges to licensure of I/O psychologists: 1) current regulations require that supervisors be licensed which is a major problem since few I/O psychologists are currently licensed and available to serve as supervisors; and, 2) the absence of any APA or APPIC accredited programs that offer pre-doctoral or post-doctoral training related to their

intended area of practice. Most other areas of concern can be, with minor changes, subsumed under the existing Supervision Guidelines. With the exceptions noted subsequently, I/O and non-HSP psychologists are expected to meet all other recommended pre-doctoral and post-doctoral supervision requirements for licensure.

Some jurisdictions have made changes in their regulations to allow greater flexibility in the requirement for I/O psychologists. Texas regulations require two full years of experience but exempt those individuals enrolled in an I/O doctoral degree program from the formal internship requirement (Rules and Regulations, Texas, 2002). Georgia regulations present detailed specifications for the licensure of I/O psychologists including requirements for supervisors who are not licensed and the criteria that must be met by a non-APA approved internship (Rules and Regulations, Georgia, 1998).

It is recommended that the following exceptions for I/O and other non-HSP psychologists be included in licensing regulations:

Psychologists whose intended area of practice is in I/O psychology or other non-HSP psychologists, who face similar problems, are exempted from the requirement that supervisors be licensed psychologists. When it can be demonstrated that a sufficient pool of licensed psychologists is available for supervision but no longer than three (3) years from the date of adoption by the jurisdiction, the licensure requirement should be reinstated. During this initial period, supervisors will be psychologists as identified by earned degrees, positions, memberships in professional organizations, publications, etc., I/O and other non-HSP psychologists may meet the 3000 (or 4000) hours of supervised experience required for licensure in settings that provide training that is consistent with the supervisee intended area of practice. At least 1500 (or 2000) hours must be completed after the granting of the doctoral degree. Training programs must be tailored to follow the general guidelines used in traditional internships and post-doctoral settings. (p. 6)

These are merely recommendations at this time but they are, at the least, an indication of efforts and successes in making supervision regulations more appropriate for non-HSPs.

OTHER SPECIAL OR CONTINUING EDUCATION COURSES

A few jurisdictions require documentation confirming that you have taken specific courses such as ethics or human sexuality to apply for licensure. Some graduate programs provide these in their curriculum, but if your program does not, these are generally offered as continuing education classes. Most jurisdictions require a certain number of continuing professional education credits (CPE) each licensure period to renew the licensure. California, for example, has a number of such courses but does exempt non-HSPs from taking some of these (e.g., child abuse or spousal abuse). It has been frustrating for non-HSP psychologists to be required to take CPE classes in areas that are outside of their area of expertise or interest. There are efforts being made to allow people to focus their continuing education in areas relevant to their practice. In the past, it was often difficult to find CPE classes that were not clinically oriented. It is now easier to find relevant CPE classes. For example, at their midwinter meetings, Division 13 (Society of Consulting Psychology) and Division 14 (Society for Industrial and Organizational Psychology) offer excellent continuing education classes. Typically APA offers continuing education classes before, during, and after its annual meeting. Some states also allow courses that can be taken through the Internet or by mail. Again, it is important to review the laws and regulations carefully. Exemptions may be hard to find because they may be located in a different section of the document. Without a careful reading, important exceptions or requirements could be missed.

Taking the Examination for Professional Practice in Psychology

There is a national test that all applicants for licensure must take called the Examination for Professional Practice in Psychology (EPPP; see chap. 4, this volume). This requirement poses no unique problems for consulting or I/O psychologists because it covers a broad range of psychology, including clinical issues, testing, social psychology, organizational psychology, research, statistics, and other topics. An I/O trained person may need to study areas that were not covered in his or her curriculum (e.g., abnormal psychology or clinical testing) but there are study materials and preparation courses that assist in this area. Although I/O people complain about the clinical items, it may be of some small comfort to know that clinically trained people complain about the number of items in the organizational area. In general, I/O people seem to do well on the test. The test is taken online by scheduling a specific time with the Prometric Testing Center.

Should you want to transfer your scores to another jurisdiction, ASPPB has a transfer service that will send on your score. In addition, it will review ASPPB's Disciplinary Data System (that notes any disciplinary actions reported by ASPPB member boards) to document your compliance to legal and ethical requirements (ASPPB, 2001, 2005). This can facilitate and speed your ability to be licensed in another jurisdiction.

OTHER TESTING

Most states or provinces currently require a jurisprudence or oral exam, or both, in addition to the EPPP (see chap. 5, this volume). Typically the jurisprudence exam covers laws and regulations of that jurisdiction and general ethics issues. In the oral exam, case studies are presented and the candidate must respond to issues raised in the example. In these situations, there is generally an oral case study option of a nonclinical nature. California, as have a number of other jurisdictions, has replaced the oral exam with a written jurisprudence exam. There are commercial study guides and courses that assist those preparing for these exams.

PRACTICING ACROSS STATE LINES

Once licensed, the particular issues for non-HSP psychologists do not end. For example, many I/O and consulting psychologists have practices that span more than one jurisdiction. This type of national (even international) practice is growing in many areas of psychology. Most jurisdictions have some short period in which an individual can work within its boundaries if licensed in another state. Unfortunately, these regulations vary enormously. In Washington, one can practice 90 days without needing to get licensed in that state. Montana has a 60-day limit. California and Ohio provide for 30 days. Louisiana also allows 30 days but requires that one is sponsored by a licensed Louisiana psychologist. Indiana requires anyone who does any work at all within that state to be licensed in Indiana.

There are a number of groups working to make these regulations more reasonable and consistent but this is a state-by-state issue. If you plan on working in any other state beyond the one in which you are getting licensed, then be sure that you check that state's regulations. Other chapters in this book describe the how to bank your academic and supervisory credentials in the ASPPB's Credential's Bank (see chap. 9, this volume). After 5 years of being licensed, you can receive the Certificate of Professional Qualification in psychology from ASPPB, or become Board Certified in Business and Consulting Psychology by the American Board of Professional Psychology (see chap. 10, this volume). These options generally make it much easier to become licensed in a new state.

Conclusion

I/O, consulting psychologists, and other non-HSPs currently need to be licensed in most states. Even before graduating, students should investigate the laws and regulations for the jurisdiction or jurisdictions in which they intend to practice. I/O or other faculty members who are preparing psychologists for practice in business need to become more aware of the licensure requirements for practitioners. Efforts to either specifically exempt non-HSPs or to make laws and regulations more appropriate for their practice should be supported.

References

Association of State and Provincial Psychology Boards, ASPPB Mobility Program. (2001). *Certificate of professional qualification in psychology.* Montgomery, AL: Author.

Association of State and Provincial Psychology Boards. (2002). *Handbook of licensing and certification requirements for psychologists in the United States and Canada.* Montgomery, AL: Author.

Association of State and Provincial Psychology Boards. (2003). *Supervision guidelines.* Retrieved May 15, 2005, from http://www.asppb. org/publications/pdf/SupervisionGuidelines.pdf

Association of State and Provincial Psychology Boards. (2005). *General mobility information.* Retrieved May 15, 2005, from http://www. asppb.org/mobility/

National Register of Health Service Providers in Psychology. (2005). *ASPPB/National Register designation project.* Retrieved May 15, 2005, from http://www.nationalregister.org/designate.htm

New York State Education Department, Office of the Professions. (2004). *Regulations of the commissioner of education: Part 72 psychology.* Retrieved May 15, 2005, from http://www.fitpsy.org/Licensing/USGuidelines/NewYork/part72.htm

Office of Licensing and Registration, Maine. (2004). *Title 32, §3811, Definition of practice of psychology.* Retrieved May 15, 2005, from http://janus.state.me.us/legis/statutes/32/title32sec3811.pdf

Tennessee Board of Examiners in Psychology. (2005). *Rules of governing psychologists* (chap. 1180-2-.01, no. 6). Retrieved January, 6, 2006, from http://www.state.tn.us/sos/rules/1180/1180-02.pdf

Ronald E. Fox

Training for Prescriptive Authority for Psychologists

14

The movement to secure prescriptive authority for psychologists grew out of the increasing professionalism of the field and rapid expansion of the scope of psychological practice (Fox, 2003). This chapter explores the development of the prescriptive authority movement for psychologists, presents reasons why prescriptive authority for psychologists is in the best interest of the public, and provides information on model curriculum and training.

Expanding Scope of Practice

The movement to include prescriptive authority as a legitimate part of psychological practice most likely began in 1981 when the American Psychological Association (APA) Board of Professional Affairs Task Force (1981) issued its famous report, *Psychologists' Use of Physical Interventions*, which not only legitimized psychologists' use of a wide variety of physical interventions, but also indicated for the first time that the profession should no longer accept an indefinite self-imposed ban on prescriptive interventions. With its growing status as a health care provider, extensive experience in treating patients on medications in collaboration with physicians, and the need for providers who could combine behavioral and medicinal treatment, additional calls for such an expansion came from several quarters over the next few years.

In 1984, U.S. Senator Daniel Inouye, in a speech to the Hawaii Psychological Association, called on the profession to seek prescriptive privileges to improve the availability of comprehensive mental health services (DeLeon, Folen, Jennings, Willis, & Wright, 1991). By 1988, there were a number of significant developments: The Division of Clinical Psychology urged training programs to develop curricula in psychopharmacology, the Division of Psychopharmacology and Substance Abuse established a committee to develop a curriculum for preparing psychologists to prescribe, the first articles in support of prescribing appeared in refereed journals, the Committee for the Advancement of Professional Practice awarded a grant to the School of Professional Psychology at Wright State University to conduct a feasibility study on training doctoral psychologists to prescribe (Buie, 1988), and it was revealed that a psychologist in the Indian Health Service had been legally prescribing for over a year with very positive results (DeLeon et al., 1991).

The U.S. Department of Defense admitted the first psychologists to an experimental program designed to train them to prescribe in the military services in 1991. The APA Board of Directors formally endorsed the project in response to attacks by various medical groups. Two years later, APA accepted a task force report outlining an educational model for three levels of psychopharmacology training: Level 1 was the basic educational background needed by all psychologists in health care; Level 2 described the training needed for competence to interact knowledgeably with physicians about their patients, and Level 3 was the training required for independent prescriptive authority. By 1995, support within the profession for adding prescriptive authority to its practice repertoire had sufficiently developed that the Council of Representatives easily passed a resolution adopting such a policy and appointing a task force to prepare both a model curriculum and model legislation for use in securing the privilege in the states. The task force's reports were approved as APA policy the following year.

The U.S. Territory of Guam and the state of New Mexico enacted legislation in 2002 enabling psychologists to prescribe. They were joined by Louisiana in 2004. Active efforts to pass similar legislation are under-way in a number of other state jurisdictions.

Importance to the Profession

Psychologists who are appropriately trained and credentialed should be allowed to prescribe because it is a logical extension of their role as experts in helping patients enhance the effectiveness of their behavior and coping skills (Fox, 1988). Modern psychological research and prac-tice has more than amply demonstrated that biomedical and behavioral factors are inextricably interwoven and that it is impossible to treat, change, or understand one without simultaneously affecting the other. Psychology needs to shed adherence to a mind–body dualism that is patently false and free itself to deal with the physical concomitants, components, and consequences of psychological events. The only limits that are acceptable are those imposed by limits in competence, not those imposed by erroneous concepts.

Prescribing by psychologists appears to be in the public interest for several reasons (Fox, 1988). First, psychologists already have most of the requisite training and skills needed to evaluate the efficacy of psychopharmacological interventions. Second, the treatment for many conditions addressed by psychologists also includes pharmacological interventions as well. Adding prescriptive authority would enable them to provide better coordinated care that is more convenient for patients than having them see two providers: one to prescribe and one to treat. Third, adding prescriptive training to the existing education of psychol-ogists would make them more highly trained than the general practice physicians who currently write the vast majority of prescriptions for mental disorders. Fourth and most important, prescriptive privileges will enable psychologists to develop the truly comprehensive and uniquely psychological treatment approaches that are greatly needed by society. Medicines are terribly important and effective, but there is still far too little knowledge about the best combination of behavioral and medicinal interventions for particular types of patients in specific types of situations. Psychology's strong research-based practice tradi-tion and its acknowledged expertise in behavioral interventions makes it uniquely positioned to become a new and much needed type of major health care provider.

Prescription Training
Should Be Postdoctoral

Experts in the field have uniformly recommended that training for pre-scriptive authority be at the postdoctoral level. The typical view, ex-pressed by McGrath et al. (2004), is that psychopharmacology training must not be done at the expense of the fundamental psychosocial educa-tion that has defined the field of psychology for more than half a century. Their view, like that of most experts in the field, is that prescriptive au-thority training is best seen as a proficiency that is obtained after the mastery and integration of the basic knowledge, attitudes, and skills of the traditional health psychologist. This is essential, it is believed, because prior training as a psychologist is critical to understanding how pharma-cological interventions best fit into the range of treatments he or she traditionally brings to each situation (Dunivin, 2003).

Other authorities, such as Sammons, Sexton, and Meredith (1996), have called attention to the fact that the basic education of psychologists is unique among the health care professions because it emphasizes many of the very areas that are either ignored or given scant attention by others. Abandoning the background that makes psychologists unique risks the loss of psychology's identity and value as a separate category of health care provider.

Psychologists must not underestimate the added value of their professional training when prescribing authority is added to their pro-fessional armamentarium. By insisting that prescribing psychologists are first trained as psychologists, they are making a very significant statement. That initial training and acculturation inevitably will shape and color subsequent training as attested to by those trained in the U.S. Department of Defense project previously mentioned (see Dunivin, 2003, for one example). Psychologists' training makes a difference in how they view and manage prescribing for their patients. As former APA President Pat DeLeon once observed, a marine who goes to law school is qualitatively different than a lawyer who enters the marines. Psychology's training is different from every other profession that has prescriptive authority and that difference is seen as highly significant.

MODEL CURRICULUM

APA's model curriculum was developed by a task force that I chaired and was subsequently approved by the Council of Representatives

(APA, 1996). It is based on a review and synthesis of several model curricula developed by such other groups as the Department of Defense demonstration project curriculum, the Blue Ribbon Panel of the Professional Education Task Force of the California Psychological Association and the California School of Professional Psychology, and the American College of Neuropsychopharmacology.

The curriculum is designed as a postdoctoral experience and intended to be an extension of the traditional doctoral training in psychology. Accordingly, the pharmacological underpinnings and clinical practices of prescribing are part of the complex set of factors influencing human psychology and reflect the integration of research and practice that is central to psychological training. Consequently, psychopharmacology training for psychologists should not merely mimic the training of physicians or pharmacists or nurses but should focus instead on behavior and coping skills. This training is intended to meet the unique needs of practicing psychologists and thus does not simply follow traditional medical practices.

Significantly, the proposed training is also supposed to include an emphasis on both the requisite knowledge in psychopharmacology as well as on the scientific methods and results on which such knowledge is based. An important goal should be to prepare psychologists to evaluate new advances in psychopharmacology research and to prepare them for lifelong learning in a field that will continue to undergo significant and rapid transformation during their years of clinical practice.

Several prerequisites are stipulated to participate in postdoctoral training:

1. A doctoral degree in psychology (e.g., Doctorate of Philosophy, Doctorate of Psychology, or Doctorate of Education).
2. Current state license as a psychologist.
3. Practice as a health services provider psychologist as defined by state law where applicable or as defined by APA.

DIDACTIC INSTRUCTION

A minimum of 300 contact hours of didactic instruction is recommended in the following core content areas:

I. Neurosciences
II. Pharmacology and psychopharmacology
III. Physiology and pathophysiology
IV. Physical and laboratory assessment
V. Clinical pharmacotherapeutics

See Table 14.1 for the recommended contact hours in each area.

TABLE 14.1

Recommended Contact Hours of Didactic Instruction in Core Content Areas

Topic	Hours
I. Neurosciences A. Neuroanatomy	25
B. Neurophysiology	25
C. Neurochemistry	25
II. Clinical and research pharmacology and psychopharmacology	
A. Pharmacology	30
B. Clinical pharmacology	30
C. Psychopharmacology	45
D. Developmental pharmacology	10
E. Chemical dependency and chronic pain management	15
III. Pathophysiology Includes normal anatomy and physiological processes as well as common pathological states, with an emphasis on how alterations in cardiovascular, renal, hepatic, gastrointestinal, neural, and endocrine functions affect bioavailability and biodisposition of drugs. This area should also address variability in drug bioavailability and disposition because of ethnic and cultural differences. The course should include normal human anatomy and physiology as well as common pathological conditions that impact the safety and efficacy of psychotherapeutic medications. Variability in response because of age, gender, disability, and ethnic differences should be addressed. Medical conditions affecting drug biodisposition and the likelihood of side effects, including contraindications for medication use, should be covered in this course.	60
IV. Introduction to physical assessment and laboratory exams (familiarity with medical charts, physical exams, laboratory and radiological examinations).	45
IV. Pharmacotherapeutics	
A. Professional, ethical, and legal issues	15
B. Psychotherapy and pharmacotherapy interactions	10
C. Computer-based aids to practice	5
D. Pharmacoepidemiology	10

CLINICAL PRACTICUM

The clinical practicum is to be an intensive, closely supervised experience involving exposure to a range of patients and diagnoses. Ideally, it will take place in both inpatient and outpatient settings, and allow the practitioner to gain exposure to acute, short-term, and maintenance medication strategies. Age, gender, disability, and ethnicity should be important factors in determining an appropriate patient mix. The trainee should treat a sufficient range and number of patients to gain experience across these dimensions. To achieve competency in treating a sufficiently diverse patient population, a minimum of 100 patients for whom the trainee assumes direct clinical responsibility or participates in case conferences should be the goal of training. The patient mix should be relevant to the psychologist's current and future practice. Additional didactics, such as the sequence in pharmacotherapeutics (see Table 14.1), may be included as seminars or colloquia during clinical training, as should additional training in physical and laboratory assessment. Supervision should be provided by qualified practitioners with demonstrated skills and experience in clinical psychopharmacology.

In summary, the clinical practicum requirements include the following elements:

- a minimum of 100 patients seen for medication;
- inpatient and outpatient placements;
- inclusion of appropriate didactic instruction; and
- a minimum of 2 hours per week of individual supervision.

PSYCHOPHARMACOLOGY EXAMINATION FOR PSYCHOLOGISTS

In 1997, APA authorized its College of Professional Psychology to develop an examination in psychopharmacology for use by licensing boards in states when prescriptive authority is granted to qualified licensed psychologists in their jurisdiction. When such laws are passed, licensing authorities will need to adopt regulations to implement the new laws. These regulations will specify the education, experience, and examination requirements for prescribing privileges. Licensing authorities will need to ensure the validity and defensibility of an examination they use as a component of a regulatory process that authorizes prescribing. The Psychopharmacology Examination for Psychologists (PEP) was carefully developed to meet this need using a methodology that complies with the highest standards for validity, fairness, and defensibility in licensing. The PEP is monitored and updated regularly to reflect changing knowledge and practice (see chap. 12, this volume).

Graduates of programs meeting the requirements of the APA model curriculum are eligible to take the exam. Scores obtained on the PEP will be "banked" in a secure database maintained by the College. Scores will be reported to state licensing authorities or to other entities on examinee authorization.

Training Programs

A number of postdoctoral training programs have been established to provide the necessary knowledge and skills to prescribe independently (Barnett & Neel, 2000). Some are partial residential programs, whereas others offer distant educational models using various combinations of distance learning and innovative electronic learning options. Some programs award a master's degree at the end of the program, whereas others give a certificate of completion. Although there is no formal recognition system to verify that a program meets APA guidelines, APA has convened a meeting of all program directors and promises to have such a process in place in the near future. Further information may be obtained from the APA Practice Directorate.

At the more basic level, the Level 1 curriculum previously mentioned has become the basic prototype of many training programs, and a number of them now offer certificates in psychopharmacology or have created a predoctoral psychopharmacology track. A few licensing boards now require basic training in psychopharmacology for all licensure candidates. Both of these trends are growing. However, the original Level 2 training (needed for active consultation with physicians) proved difficult to distinguish from that needed for actual prescribing and as such has been incorporated into the basic psychopharmacology training.

Conclusion

Psychology's research-based practice tradition and acknowledged expertise in behavioral interventions provide the basis for continued investigation into the best combination of behavioral and medical interventions. With this unique training, it is in the best interest of both the profession and the public for psychologists who are properly trained and credentialed to be licensed to consult with other practitioners on medication issues, and to prescribe medications for their own patients.

References

American Psychological Association. (1996). *Recommended postdoctoral training in psychopharmacology for prescribing privileges.* Washington, DC: Author.

American Psychological Association Task Force on Psychologists' Use of Physical Interventions. (1981). *Psychologists' use of physical interventions.* Washington, DC: American Psychological Association.

Barnett, J., & Neel, M. (2000). Must all psychologists study psychopharmacology? *Professional Psychology: Research and Practice, 31,* 619–627.

Buie, J. (1988). Practice priorities: Medicare amendments, hospital privileges, HMO reforms, prescription privileges? *Monitor on Psychology,* 7, 14–15.

DeLeon, P. H., Folen, R. A., Jennings, F. L., Willis, D. J., & Wright, R. H. (1991). The case for prescription privileges: A logical evolution of professional practice. *Journal of Clinical Child Practice, 20,* 254–267.

Dunivin, D. L. (2003). Experiences of a Department of Defense prescribing psychologist: A personal account. In M. T. Sammons, R. F. Levant, & R. U. Paige (Eds.), *Prescriptive authority for psychologists: A history and guide* (pp. 103–115). Washington, DC: American Psychological Association.

Fox, R. E. (1988). Prescription privileges: Their implications for the practice of psychology. *Psychotherapy, 25,* 501–507.

Fox, R. E. (2003). Early efforts by psychologists to obtain prescriptive authority. In M. T. Sammons, R. F. Levant, & R. U. Paige (Eds.), *Prescriptive authority for psychologists: A history and guide* (pp. 33–45). Washington, DC: American Psychological Association.

McGrath, R., Wiggins, J., Sammons, M., Levant, R., Brown, A., & Stock, W. (2004). Professional issues in pharmacotherapy for psychologists. *Professional Psychology: Research and Practice, 35,* 158–163.

Sammons, M., Sexton, J., & Meredith, J. (1996). Basic science training in psychopharmacology: How much is enough. *American Psychologist, 51,* 230–234.

Karen S. Vaughn and Gerald K. Gentry

Do No Harm

15

Unlike many physicians, psychologists do not have to swear to a Hippocratic Oath; there is an inherent social and ethical contract that psychologists will do no harm. Although the words "First, do no harm" are not actually in the Hippocratic Oath, in his writings, Hippocrates focused on the need both to protect patients from harm and to not cause harm (Hippocratic oath, 2004). American Psychological Association's (APA) "Ethical Principles of Psychologists and Code of Conduct" (2002, Principle A: Beneficence and Nonmaleficence) states that "Psychologists strive to benefit those with whom they work and take care to do no harm."

It is important to keep in mind that the purpose of all of the guidelines and requirements outlined in this book is the legislators' concern about protection of the public. The laws and rules were established to make sure that minimal educational and training standards for the practice of psychology are obtained. Also, toward this end, students spend years in making sure that their education, training, and experience meet the criteria for licensure as a psychologist.

Once a license is obtained, the concern is how one practices psychology, ethically and legally, such that consumers are not harmed. Robert Kinscherff, former chair of APA's Ethics Committee which adjudicates ethics complaints, encourages psychologists to think about ethics as a way to be better in their practice rather than worrying about getting in trouble. "Good ethical practice is good professional practice, which is good risk management practice" (Smith, 2003, p. 50)

To assure familiarity with the state or province's laws, one will most likely be required to take a jurisprudence examination after approval of one's application and passage of the Examination for Professional Practice in Psychology (EPPP). Jurisprudence exams cover the laws and rules pertaining to the provision of psychological services including laws governing mandated reporting of child abuse, child custody laws and elder abuse laws, informed consent, release of information, confidentiality, and so forth. Not only does one need to be very familiar with this information to pass the exam; it is the candidate's responsibility to keep current concerning any changes to licensure laws and other state and provincial laws that pertain to the provision of psychological services. A psychologist's attempt to plead "I didn't know the laws had changed" is indefensible (see chap. 5, this volume).

In addition to these laws, the practice of psychology is also governed by ethical principles to which one must adhere. Codes of ethics and professional conduct are published by the APA and can also be accessed online at http://www.apa.org/ethics/ the Association of State and Provincial Psychology Boards (ASPPB) and are located at http://www.asppb.org/pubs/code.asp; and the Canadian Psychological Association, whose codes can be found at http://www.cpa.ca/cpasite/userfiles/Documents/Canadian%20Code%2of%20Ethics%20for%20Psycho.pdf. The APA "Ethical Principles of Psychologists and Code of Conduct" may also be downloaded in .pdf format at http://www.apa.org/ethics/code2002.pdf (APA, 2002). In addition, codes of ethics as well as practice guidelines are published by specialties or APA divisions. A jurisdiction's laws and rules may include one or the other, if not both, of these ethical standards in their entirety, in part, or by reference. The APA Ethics Code was revised in 2002, effective June, 2003 as was the ASPPB Code of Conduct in 2005 (ASPPB, 2005).

Maintaining familiarity and staying current with these codes of ethics and practicing accordingly is essential. The consequences for violating laws, rules, or ethical standards may be severe regardless of sanction. If these standards are violated, then not only is there a danger of having action taken against a license but also the psychologist may be required to appear before APA's Ethics Committee or similar ethics committees in the jurisdiction or region in which the violation occurred. If a licensing board takes action against a license, then such action will be reported to the Association of State and Provincial Psychology Board's Disciplinary Data System (DDS). "The DDS of ASPPB is the agency charged with recording, classifying, disseminating, and coordinating disciplinary data. The system provides a history of both the types of violations committed by psychologists and the range of penalties or sanctions meted out by licensure boards" (Kirkland, Kirkland, & Reaves, 2004, p.180). However, "both the American Psychological Association (APA) and the ASPPB keep track of sanctions in terms of ethical violations and disciplinary dispositions, respectively" (Kirkland et al., 2004, p. 180).

The DDS that is maintained by ASPPB is the largest accumulation of data pertaining to sanctions taken against the licenses of psychologists in North America. It is directly linked with the transfer of a psychologist's EPPP score from one jurisdiction to another, as well as to one's application for the ASPPB credentials bank or Certificate of Professional Qualification in psychology. This process was instituted by ASPPB to keep unscrupulous psychologists, who have had discipline against their license, from moving to another jurisdiction in an attempt to avoid disciplinary action.

It is important to avoid committing violations not only so that there is not a report sent to the DDS but also because insurance companies and managed care contracts ask specifically if there has been a "complaint filed against your license." A few may ask whether the complaint resulted in a license being restricted in any way, but most ask whether there has been any complaint filed. A "yes" response will require explanation and may have an adverse affect on one's practice, whether or not the complaint was found to have merit.

ASPPB publishes a "Top Ten" list of reasons that licensees have been disciplined (see Table 15.1). These are fairly broad categories and, especially the first two items, contain a considerable range of reasons for action taken.

Because ASPPB's "Top Ten" reflects broad categories, within which numerous different violations may be recorded, there are specifics within these categories of which all practitioners should be aware. Randolph P. Reaves, long-time CEO and General Counsel for the ASPPB, authored an excellent treatise entitled *Avoiding Liability in Mental Health Practice* (Reaves, 2001). He expertly outlined with accompanying legal references potential problems in the areas of civil, criminal, and license-related liability. His book is a valuable resource and offers a number of practical ideas for positive actions to avoid liability.

The authors of this chapter offer the following additional affirmative thoughts gleaned from our combined 30-plus years working as psychology regulators. We attempt to provide an overview of some useful ways to ensure that those individuals being served are not affected negatively, even if inadvertently, and also ways of keeping out of trouble. The resources listed herein can provide valuable information for any practitioner.

TABLE 15.1

Reported Disciplinary Actions for Psychologists, August 1983 to December 2004

Reason for action	Number disciplined
Sexual/dual relationship with patient	842
Unprofessional/unethical/negligent practice	823
Conviction of crimes	252
Fraudulent acts	173
Improper/inadequate record keeping	148
Breach of confidentiality	124
Inadequate or improper supervision	121
Failure to comply with continuing education requirements	121
Impairment	108
Fraud in application for license	50
Total	2,762[a]

Note. Compiled from actions reported to the Association of State and Provincial Psychology Boards (ASPPB) Disciplinary Data System by ASPPB member boards. [a]The difference in the total number of reported disciplinary actions (3,303) and this total is that some jurisdictions do not report reasons or the reason reported does not fall into one of the categories listed.

AVOID DUAL RELATIONSHIPS

Probably one of the most debated and difficult to define falls under the category of dual relationships. "A central question in any multiple relationship situations is, whose needs are being met here?" noted Stephen Behnke, Director of APA's Ethics Office, which advises psychologists on ethical dilemmas. "Whenever the answer is the needs of the psychologist, that's a time when the psychologist needs to take great care and get a consultation" (Smith, 2003, p. 50).

Do not become involved in a dual role in custody or divorce matters by providing service as the treating psychologist and the reporting psychologist. "Therapeutic contact with the child or involved participants following a child protection evaluation is discouraged and when done, is undertaken with caution" (APA Committee on Professional Practice and Standards, 1998, sect. II, no. 8). This does not mean that one cannot testify on a client's behalf in a court proceeding. This is an area in which it may be important to obtain legal advice. The bottom line that regulators and ethics committees evaluate is whether the relationship appears to have exploited the client in any way. This judgment, however, is relative to whether the client was exploited, regardless of differing viewpoints on the matter.

In the last decade or so, regulators and ethics committees have realized that in rural communities, there may be no way to escape treating someone from a local bank, car dealership, or common church. However, if one's practice is not in a rural or otherwise limited community, these relationships should be avoided. If an error is made, err to the side of caution in these matters.

Power

There is always an inherent power imbalance in the therapeutic relationship whether one perceives it to be present or not. Clients look to their psychologist as the authority and the expert; therefore, professional boundaries must always be maintained. How much of a power differential exists between the psychologist and the client is the key. The greater the difference, the more care should be taken.

Power differentials occur outside the therapeutic relationship as well. There is a difference in power between faculty and students, supervisor and intern. Even students providing supervision or teaching undergraduate students need to be mindful of the power inequities.

Sex With Clients

One type of multiple relationship is never acceptable: "Sexual relationships with current clients are never permissible," noted Behnke (Smith, 2003, p. 51). Although sexual relationships with previous clients are not automatic violations of the Ethics Code if they occur more than 2 years after terminating therapy, "psychologists need to be mindful of the harm that can come from a sexual involvement with a client no matter when it occurs," Behnke added (p. 51). The APA Ethics Code is very clear on the matter of sexual relations with a client. It also prohibits a client–therapist relationship between psychologists and anyone with whom they have previously engaged in any sexually intimate behavior (Koocher & Keith-Spiegel, 1998).

FOCUS ON ONE'S PRIVATE LIFE

At ASPPB's 34th Annual Meeting of Delegates in Scottsdale, Arizona, in 1994, Susan Cave presented the characteristics of their disciplined psychologists in New Mexico. The board discovered many private lives in disarray—relationship difficulties, financial liabilities, loneliness, and isolation. The 44th Annual Meeting in 2004 revisited the issues of wellness and impairment. A study conducted by Pope (1993) found that 90% of the offenders reported being vulnerable, needy, or lonely. These "high-need states were related to unsatisfying marriages, recent separations, and/or divorces" (p. 347). Research suggests that marital status may be an important variable. A study of sexually exploited patients found that "severity of impacts can be predicted by . . . the marital status of the practitioner" (Feldman-Summers & Jones, as cited in Pope, 1993, p. 374). Another example of vulnerability involved an occupant of Kansas' death row, who complained to one of the chapter authors about a previous counselor who might have helped prevent a murder: "He spent more time talking about his problems than he did talking about mine!"

Time set aside for self, family, and friends should be jealously guarded. It is extremely important to establish and maintain boundaries between personal life and work. Hobbies that may have been set aside during graduate school could be pursued to create balance to one's life. The occasional break from the stresses of a practice, such as travel, helps to not only maintain balance but also keep perspective by getting away. We have all heard the instructions from the airline flight attendant, "Place your oxygen mask on first, then assist those who may need assistance." One cannot be effective as a professional if he or she is not taking care of self first.

STAY INVOLVED AND CONNECTED

Our experience, as regulators, has been that isolation is related to poor judgment and potential discipline. A disproportionate percentage of disciplined psychologists are not active members of professional associations. Psychologists are well advised to join and maintain membership in metropolitan, state, regional, and national organizations. These associations offer valuable opportunities for professional and personal support, as well as training and continuing education credits. If in a solo practice, joining or forming a peer supervision group can be invaluable. Such a group can offer support and encouragement as well as accountability, therapeutic opinions, and suggestions for treating difficult clients. Joining a group-specific electronic mailing list can offer additional arenas for discussion and input. These avenues can assist in sustaining one's self professionally.

TAKE CARE OF BUSINESS

Some professions require their students to take courses with such titles as "How To Start and Operate a Small Business." This seems wise for the profession of psychology to emulate given the number of disciplinary actions whose foundation lies in flawed business practices. Unfortunately, the coursework demands in psychology programs offer little opportunity for such electives. Most new practitioners acquire their business acumen on their own time and at their own expense. A prudent newly licensed psychologist starting out should consider finding a business mentor. Community colleges may offer courses in entrepreneurship or sound business practices. There is a wealth of information available from the U.S. Small Business Administration. They offer not only help and guidelines for starting and maintaining a business but also online courses, free workshops, and seminars on business-related topics. Their assistance is available at http://www.sba.gov/ and http://www.sba.gov/training.

When in Doubt

When in doubt about an ethical dilemma, seeking another opinion from a colleague or expert is prudent. When in doubt about a legal issue, the advice of an attorney may be needed. Consultation with a colleague who may have more experience or specialty training is always a good idea. Documenting the consultation can add additional support if needed. Discussing matters pertaining to clients with a peer review group, disguising any identifying information, and documenting that it was discussed along with the consensus of the peer group can offer support as well as substantiation of professional behavior in a difficult case or action.

Stay Within One's Scope of Practice

Practice within one's areas of education, training, and supervised experience. Primarily, this would be the coursework that was obtained in a formal education program. It may also be the result of an internship or postdoctoral training under supervision. Attending a great workshop or seminar may be informational and even helpful, but be sure that competence is established in any new or experimental practice or procedures. It may be advisable to obtain additional academic classes or operate under the supervision of a psychologist who is proficient in the new technique until your skills are well established.

Renew Licenses on Time

Obtain information from the licensing board to be sure of the time that licenses are due for renewal and the grace period, if there is one. If a license lapses, then you may find that statutes and rules may have changed since the time of original licensure. This could result in having to go through the application procedure again, and this time, one may not qualify for licensure because of evolving requirements. Also, allowing a license to lapse can raise questions about ethical practice.

Take Care of Continuing Professional Education Credits

Do not underestimate this one. It is easy to get busy and not pay attention to whether one is meeting a jurisdiction's CPE requirements.

However, failure to complete the required number of continuing education credits is cause for discipline against or suspension of a license that may result in a report being filed with ASPPB's DDS. At an annual meeting of ASPPB, Randolph P. Reaves postulated that he could foresee the day when failure to complete continuing education credits could top the ASPPB's "Top Ten" reasons for licensees being disciplined.

Keep Business and Personal Life Separate

Do not involve clients in any business or financial contract or arrangement, such as a personal make-up or home products business or one of a friend or relative. Do not participate in any financial investments with a client in either direction. Clients should not be asked to invest in any business endeavor nor should psychologists involve themselves in any client's business venture. Do not discuss one's personal life and problems with clients. Doing so is not self-disclosure that is in any way helpful to the client but is a violation of professional boundaries.

Document, Document, Document

Not only is failure to keep accurate records a common cause for discipline, client records are a valuable source of information if one is called on to defend actions in a disciplinary action. Contacts made, what was said or recommended, as well as any contact or input from a professional consultation with a peer review group, attorney, colleague, or expert can prove invaluable. Again, consulting the ethical principles and codes of ethics mentioned within this chapter provides valuable information about what should be kept in client records and how this information should be maintained and disposed.

Confidentiality

"Ask yourself, 'On what basis am I making this disclosure?'" advises Behnke (Smith, 2003, p. 51). "Is there a law that mandates the disclosure? Is there a law that permits me to disclose? Has my client consented to the disclosure?" he adds. APA's 2002 Ethics Code stipulates that psychologists may only disclose the minimum information necessary to provide needed services; obtain appropriate consultations; protect the client, psychologist, or others from harm; or obtain payment for services from a client (Smith, 2003).

Sound Practice

Never make diagnostic statements or references about anyone that has not been personally seen and evaluated professionally. In addition, if treatment is provided to a child whose parents are divorced, it is always a good idea to obtain and keep on file a copy of the divorce decree. Be knowledgeable about what information the respective parents are entitled to. For example, one of the authors, while in private practice, obtained the divorce decree of the parents of a child in treatment. The noncustodial parent's attorney had included a statement in the decree allowing his client full access to what was discussed by his son in therapy as well as discussions with the custodial parent. This resulted in lengthy and time-consuming conversations among parents and attorneys to arrive at agreeable guidelines for the sharing of information. The decree can, and usually does, contain specific information about visitation, financial responsibilities, access to information, and other particulars that may come up as an issue in therapy.

Conclusion

This chapter is not meant to serve as an exhaustive reference for avoiding liability for the new practitioner. There are entire books written on this topic, and the codes of ethics and conduct listed in this chapter are extensive. A good general reference that gives case examples is *Ethics in Psychology, Professional Standards and Cases* written by Gerald P. Koocher and Patricia Keith-Spiegel (1998). *Ethical Conflicts in Psychology* (3rd ed.) edited by Donald N. Bersoff (2003) presents real-life ethical dilemmas and their resolutions. *Ethics in Psychotherapy and Counseling* (Kenneth S. Pope and Melba Jean Trinidad Vasquez, 2000) is another very good resource for ethical practice.

We have provided some resources and practical, positive steps that may be taken to avoid liability by tending to one's practice and personal life. Instituting these suggestions may help the new practitioner to be aware of some of the pitfalls and assist in establishing a sound professional practice.

References

American Psychological Association. (2002). Ethical principles of psychologists and code of conduct. *American Psychologist, 47*, 1597–1611. Also available from APA's Web site, http://www.apa.org/ethics/code2002.html#principle_a

American Psychological Association, Committee on Professional Practice and Standards. (1998). *Guidelines for psychological evaluations in child protection matters* (sect. II, no. 8). Retrieved February 8, 2006, from http://www.apa.org/practice/childprotection.html

Association of State and Provincial Psychology Boards. (2005). *ASPPB code of conduct.* Retrieved January 29, 2006, from http://www.asppb.org/publications/model/conduct.aspx

Canadian Psychological Association. (2000). *Canadian code of ethics for psychologists* (3rd ed.). Retrieved March 22, 2006, from http://www.cpa.ca/cpasite/userfiles/Documents/Canadian%20Code%20of%20Ethics%20for%20Psycho.pdf

Hippocratic oath. (2004). *Encyclopædia Britannica.* Retrieved January 29, 2006, from http://www.britannica.com/eb/article?tocId=9040542

Kirkland, K., Kirkland, K. L., & Reaves, R. P. (2004). On the professional use of disciplinary data. *Professional Psychology: Research and Practice, 35,* 179–184.

Koocher, G. P., & Keith-Spiegel, P. (1998). *Ethics in psychology: Professional standards and cases* (2nd ed.). New York: Oxford University Press.

Pope, K. S. (1993). Licensing disciplinary actions for psychologists who have been sexually involved with a client: Some information about offenders. *Professional Psychology: Research and Practice, 24,* 374–377.

Reaves, R. P. (2001). *Avoiding liability in mental health practice.* Montgomery, AL: Association of State and Provincial Psychology Boards.

Smith, D. (2003, January). 10 ways practitioners can avoid frequent ethical pitfalls. *Monitor on Psychology, 34,* 50.

U.S. Small Business Administration. (n.d.). *Small business training network.* Retrieved January 29, 2006, from http://www.sba.gov/training

Raymond D. Fowler and Russell S. Newman

Future Trends in Professional Psychology

16

Predicting the future is a hazardous enterprise. In 1864, Victor Hugo predicted that the invention of a flying machine would result in abolition of war, and a French military officer of that period opined that the airplane would be fine for sport, but it would have no effect on transportation, communication, or the military.

The health disciplines have not been immune to predictions from clouded crystal balls. For example, various new developments in mental health care over the years—electroconvulsive therapy, lobotomy, psychotropic drugs—have led to predictions that soon there would be no role for psychologists and other mental health professionals. In 1964 a president of the American Psychological Association (APA) announced the death of clinical psychology, which, despite its obituary, has continued to grow and prosper.

So it is with some trepidation that we attempt to look ahead and predict where the profession of psychology might be in 2025. First, we look at the current status of psychology as a discipline and as a profession, and then examine trends likely to influence professional psychology in the next two decades.

Status of Psychology
as a Discipline

In little more than a century, psychology has grown into a large and robust discipline. In the United States, there are about 115,000 psychologists (National Science Foundation, 2004). Psychology is by far the largest and most influential of the behavioral sciences. In most colleges and universities, psychology is the most popular elective course and ranks among the top two or three undergraduate majors (Sax et al., 2005). The number of doctoral programs has doubled in the past decade, and there are still many applicants for each available position (APA, 2005).

It seems to us that employment prospects for psychology students are quite good. Graduates with majors in psychology find employment in the public and private sectors in such fields as social services, sales, personnel work, public relations, and management. Doctoral-level graduates have a broad range of opportunities, especially in educational, public service, and health care settings. Most doctoral students find employment before or soon after graduation, and the rate of unemployment in psychology is very low. The continuing demand for psychology courses at the undergraduate level and the large number of students applying for graduate work suggests that psychology as a discipline will continue to prosper in the years ahead.

Status of Psychology
as a Profession

About 90,000 psychologists are licensed to practice in the United States, most as health care practitioners (Association of State and Provincial Psychology Boards, 2002). The range of practice opportunities continues to expand, especially as more psychologists enter underserved sectors such as geriatrics and underserved places such as rural and inner-city America. Potential opportunities in the field of general health are likely to be far greater, in the future, than in mental health, and the increased recognition of psychology as a comprehensive health profession reflects a growing interest in applying psychological knowledge to the prevention and treatment of physical illness.

Some psychologists believe that there is an oversupply of practicing psychologists in the United States. To the extent that psychologists limit themselves to traditional mental health practice, the concern has some validity. However, as psychologists continue to diversify their practices beyond mental health, particularly into the general health arena, many more employment opportunities will be available to psychologists.

Economic Factors Likely to Affect Professional Practice

Due in large part to concerns about the costs of health care over the last 20 years, economic factors have begun to exert considerable influence on the delivery of health care services, including the practice of psychology. Market forces and efforts to contain costs through managed care have made the private independent practice of psychology more challenging and have reduced the income of virtually all health care practitioners. Psychologists in the public sector have also been significantly affected by economic factors as state and federal budget deficits have led to a reduction of funding for mental health services in hospitals, prisons, and community facilities (Kaiser Permanente, 2005). To attempt to predict the continuing impact of economic factors on the practice of psychology of the future, it is important to first have some understanding of how these factors have come about.

Concern about the detrimental affect of spiraling health care costs in the early 1990s prompted legislative efforts to reform the health care system, most notably the Clinton Health Security Act of 1994. Although the Clinton proposal for government legislated reform was not enacted by Congress, it led to considerable changes in the private health care market and fueled unfettered competition in efforts to decrease the cost of health care services. Managed care techniques to contain costs by limiting services, techniques which had been around since the early 1970s but little used, became a popular method for employers and insurers in the context of private market reform.

During this period, the health care industry was evolving from a fragmented cottage industry to an increasingly consolidated industry dominated by large health care corporations such as hospital and managed care companies. Integrated delivery systems—networks that provide a coordinated continuum of services—became popular. Employers and other third-party payers of health care services could now arrange for many different services to be provided by a relatively small number of contracts within an integrated delivery system.

For psychologists, changes in the health care marketplace have meant a growing importance for diversification of services; psychologists who could provide a wider range of services would be more competitive. As a result, individual psychologists are increasingly offering services beyond traditional psychotherapy and assessment for mental health patients. Sports psychology, forensic psychology, executive coaching, and gerontology, for example, are areas into which many psychologists have expanded their practices. Group practices that combine a number of areas within the diverse discipline of psychology (e.g., pediatric, child, adolescent, adult, family, neuropsychology, and rehabilitation) also provide a way for psychologists to be more competitive in the transforming health care marketplace. Groups that provide a range of psychological services and that also link with primary care physicians further optimize their ability to provide a diverse range of services. The trend toward diversification, already influencing training patterns, is likely to continue well into the future.

Scope of Practice in Professional Psychology

By definition and tradition, a profession is self-regulating and determines its own scope of practice within the legal framework in which it operates. Despite sometimes strenuous efforts on the part of organized psychiatry, professional psychology has steadily expanded its scope of practice over the years and has achieved full autonomy and legal recognition throughout the United States. It seems probable that psychology's scope of practice will continue to expand, especially in those areas such as prescribing or others that interface with the medical profession.

PSYCHOLOGY AS A HEALTH CARE PROFESSION

Until the 1990s, the practice of psychology and the policy development to support it have focused heavily on mental health services. For a great many years, clinical training was relatively narrow, and some practitioners still limit themselves to only a few traditional activities: individual psychotherapy, psychological assessment, and occasional consultation. Although practitioners with well-established practices and referral networks may be able to continue to limit themselves to these few functions, new graduates who do not diversify their services will have difficulty establishing themselves in a somewhat crowded field. Increasingly, psychologists, particularly newer psychologists, are developing practices that involve applying their skills beyond mental health to the broader area of general health.

This is not to say that psychologists have not previously been involved in health care apart from mental health. Health psychologists, neuropsychologists, and rehabilitation psychologists, for example, have for some time worked in areas beyond mental health. It has been true, however, that most practicing psychologists, particularly those in independent practice, have historically been primarily engaged in assessment and treatment of people with mental health disorders.

Since the 1990s, however, more psychologists have been viewing psychology as a comprehensive health profession with the ability to provide services to people with health disorders as well as to people with mental health disorders. In fact, practicing in the health arena is already a significant trend for the profession. Psychologists are increasingly focusing on the psychosocial contributors and consequences of physical disease, as well as on the application of psychological and behavioral technologies to the treatment of various medical problems (see Newman & Reed, 1997). Psychological services integrated into the treatment of breast cancer, cardiovascular disease, essential hypertension, diabetes, and asthma are just a few examples.

In 2002 the APA Practice Directorate worked with the American Medical Association to create six new reimbursement codes under the Current Procedural Terminology coding system, termed the *health and behavior assessment and intervention codes*. These new codes cover psychological services delivered to patients with physical health diagnoses. This new development has both followed the trend of psychologists providing services to people with physical disorders and has further stimulated it as well.

Psychology's pursuit of the authority to prescribe medication is also consistent with expanding into a comprehensive health profession (see chap. 14, this volume). To date, New Mexico, Louisiana, and Guam have enacted prescriptive authority laws, and legislation has been introduced in 16 additional states. The Department of Defense (DoD) Psychopharmacology Demonstration Project provided strong evidence that appropriately trained psychologists can prescribe safely and effectively. As a result of the DoD program, specially trained psychologists have been prescribing in the military for more than a decade. Some psychologists are also prescribing, with limited formularies, to treat obesity or to facilitate smoking cessation. Psychologists authorized to prescribe do not simply become prescription writers; with prescriptive authority, psychologists are able to add the use of medication to their already existing wide range of psychological intervention strategies.

The successful efforts in Guam, New Mexico, and Louisiana, if followed by more successes in other jurisdictions, could increase the momentum toward nationwide prescriptive authority. In the words of Senator Daniel K. Inouye who first encouraged the psychologists of Hawaii to pursue prescriptive authority, " . . . when you have obtained this statutory authority, you will have really made the big time. Then, you truly will be an autonomous (health) profession and your clients will be well served" (Inouye, 1984, p. 7).

The future of prescriptive authority for psychologists depends largely on the advocacy of state psychological associations. Efforts to enact such legislation are costly, time consuming, and face many obstacles, especially the determined and well-financed opposition of psychiatry. It will happen, but it is an evolutionary process that may take a long time.

PSYCHOLOGY'S ROLE IN PREVENTION

Another expanded role for psychology in the future will be in the area of health promotion and prevention. Most of the progress in health care has always come from prevention, but prevention has never been a priority for funding. Smedley and Syme (2000, as cited in DeLeon, Hagglund, Ragusea, & Sammons, 2003) noted: "The vast majority of the nation's health research resources have traditionally been directed toward biomedical research endeavors, with less than 5% of the approximately $1 trillion spent annually on health care in the nation being devoted to reducing risks posed by preventable conditions" (p. 557). Prevention, which almost always involves changes in lifestyle and health habits, is the natural domain of psychologists. Changing the behaviors that often lead to illness, impaired functioning, and premature mortality is a complex challenge for which psychologists are uniquely qualified by training and experience. Obesity, AIDS, diabetes, heart disease, drug addiction, and a host of other conditions grow out of and are exacerbated by behaviors that are, at least in principle, subject to modification. It is likely that psychologists, as they demonstrate their skills in behavior change, will be increasingly called on to serve on the front lines of disease prevention.

Psychology's involvement in health promotion is likely to be further fueled by the fact that, more than ever, lifestyle and behavior are being recognized as important factors in physical health and physical illness. For example, the U.S. Congress observed that "obesity has become our nation's fastest rising public health threat with the disease affecting nearly one-third of the adult American population" (S. Rep. No. 108-81, 2003, p. 7). The Senate also reported that the dramatic increase in obesity is particularly associated with a nationwide increase in diabetes, a disease also implicated in other serious health problems such as heart disease and blindness. Prevention through lifestyle and behavior change is perhaps the best weapon against these problems. The implications of this recognition for psychology are profound. Psychologists, who are experts (perhaps the experts) in behavior, have much to offer in this arena and will be increasingly recognized as important members of teams of professionals working to prevent chronic disease, as well as engaging in disease management when diseases occur.

DEMOGRAPHIC CHANGES THAT WILL AFFECT PROFESSIONAL PSYCHOLOGY

This is a period of rapidly changing demographics that will have profound effects on psychology and the nation. The face of the profession of psychology is changing as is the face of America. Two of these demographic changes are reviewed subsequently.

Gender

Psychology, like many other professions, has seen a steady change in gender composition. Once mostly the province of men, the ratio of men to women in psychology is now close to even (American Psychological Association, 1995). Yet the increasing number of women who major in psychology, continue for doctoral work, and enter the field, especially in professional psychology, suggest that by 2025, most psychologists will be women (National Science Foundation, 2003). Fears that the "feminization" of psychology will lead to lowered status and reduced compensation are based on developments in fields such as teaching, nursing, and secretarial work and may not apply to doctoral-level professions.

Racial and Ethnic Diversity

The traditional pattern of White psychologists seeing mostly White clients is undergoing changes that are likely to increase in the coming decades. The diversity of psychology students and practitioners is increasing, but much more slowly than the diversity of the general population (Leong, Kohout, Smith, & Wicherski, 2003). Hispanics, Asians, and African Americans in particular, represent a growing percentage of the U.S. population, and it is likely that they will be increasingly represented among the clientele of psychologists. The growing social presence of diverse groups in the larger society will mandate a higher degree of cultural sensitivity among psychologists. Although some individuals prefer to be seen by psychologists who are culturally similar to them, psychologists who are well trained and culturally competent are not limited to clients of their own racial and ethnic groups. Psychologists can increase the effectiveness and acceptability of their services if they carefully adhere to the *Guidelines for Providers of Psychological Services to Ethnic, Linguistic, and Culturally Diverse Populations* (APA, 1990). Fluency in the language of the population most likely to be seen in one's practice is also highly desirable.

OTHER EXTERNAL FACTORS INFLUENCING PSYCHOLOGISTS' FUTURE DIRECTIONS

The practice of psychology will be affected by new developments in the Internet and information technology as well as by the growing consumer empowerment phenomenon in the United States. With rapid developments in professional psychology now taking place in other countries, the psychologist of the future will be part of the globalization of psychology.

Internet and Information Technology

The Internet explosion and the development of new information technologies are also beginning to have an impact on healthcare, an industry considered by some to be the most information-intensive sector of the economy (U.S. Government Accountability Office, 2005). One important technology issue for psychology will be determining under what conditions, with which services, and for what types of problems these new technologies will facilitate the delivery of psychological services. Some disorders and some people may be well served by using the Internet to facilitate their treatment, whereas others may not. This is an empirical and experiential question that is just now in the process of being asked and answered. Eventually, it is likely that Internet and telehealth interventions will become simply additional media that are available to be used, when appropriate, to help deliver psychological services.

Another issue influencing the practice of psychology will be the impact of the Internet and information technologies on the structure and reform of the health care system. Over the last 10 years, since about 1995, efforts to decrease the cost of health care have relied on decreasing utilization through increased administrative activity. The result is that Americans are still spending 15% of the gross national product on health care (Levit et al., 2004), and administrative costs have continued to rise. A reported 44 million Americans are without health insurance (Mills & Bhandari, 2003) and other barriers to accessing quality care exist as well. Most agree that market-driven managed health care has failed to solve the problems it was intended to address and has created new problems within health care. Yet, there is little consensus as to what new solutions might be successful.

The Internet and new information technologies offer one alternative by focusing on reducing administrative activities and costs. Electronic claims processing, electronic record keeping, and using the Internet's capacity to disseminate information to create truly informed consumers of health care are but a few of the possibilities for creating a more efficient, less costly health care system. Psychologists of the future will need to be able to use these information technologies to be full participants in the health care system.

Consumer Impact

Consumer empowerment, a virtual mantra of the baby boomer generation, is likely to converge with the Internet to influence health care and psychologists. Some large employers have already begun experimenting with a new type of health plan for their employees, termed *consumer-directed health care* (Gabel, Lo Sasso, & Rice, 2002). Under this type of plan, employees receive an annual allocation of available funds from their employers, ranging from $1,000 to $2000, to be paid out only as used. These funds, sometimes called a health savings account (HSA), can be used to pay for plan deductibles, copayments for IRS-qualified healthcare expenses, or to purchase other health insurance coverage, including even long-term care coverage. Unused funds can be rolled over into future years and added to the annual HSA allocation. Consumer choice of services will be heavily influenced by health information available on the Internet. When the HSA funds are exhausted, the employee is responsible for expenses up to the deductible amount for a catastrophic plan; that is, a plan whose coverage does not start until some relatively high dollar amount has been reached, and then covers most care in full. This type of consumer-directed plan is likely to become increasingly popular over the next decade.

It is important that services considered by the plan to be preventive, such as physicals or mammograms, are covered by the plan in total, at any time. In this context, it will be critical that psychologists' preventive services, such as stress management, be recognized by employers as preventive services. Otherwise, employees will be forced to pay out-of-pocket and will likely be less inclined to seek those services. Similarly, consumer-directed plans can also provide services that are consistent with appropriate management of certain diseases. In this scenario, for example, employees would have an extra incentive to seek psychological services to aid in the management of diabetes or asthma, assuming the employer recognized psychological services as part of the disease management of those disorders. Just as changes in the health care system over the last decade have encouraged psychologists to engage in health promotion, prevention, and disease management, so too will changes over the next decade.

International Developments

Along with the development of the global economy has come the globalization of psychology. Once thought of as an American phenomenon, it appears to us that the professional practice of psychology is now in most of the countries of the world in various stages of development. The explosive growth in professional psychology, which took place in the United States several decades ago, is now taking place in many parts of the world. As recently as 1985, more than half of the psychologists in the world were in the United States, but now Europe has far more professional psychologists than the United States. Brazil has almost as many, and the sleeping giants of Asia, China, and India are just beginning their period of growth. By 2025, more than 80% of the world's psychologists will be outside of the United States, and significant developments in practice may come from any part of the world. Many psychology departments are already internationalizing their curricula, and more will be doing so soon. It is important now, and will be even more important in the future, for American psychologists to be aware of and understand developments in the rest of the world.

WHERE ARE WE LIKELY TO BE IN 2025?

On the basis of what we know today and extrapolating to the future from past developments and current trends, we make the following fearless predictions:

1. Psychology as a discipline will continue to prosper. A steady flow of highly qualified students will continue. University-based comprehensive psychology departments will continue to supply most of the psychologists in areas other than health care, but an increasing number of health care psychologists will graduate from the professional schools of psychology.
2. The number of licensed psychologists will continue its steady increase. Fewer new psychologists will narrowly specialize

in psychotherapy and mental health; more will diversify their practices, especially in general health areas. More opportunities will arise in specialties such as geriatrics, health, and wellness promotion, and more psychologists will provide services to underserved communities and individuals.

3. More third-party payers will reimburse for prevention and health promotion as the nation becomes increasingly conscious of the relationship of health habits to longevity and continued health, and psychologists will play a leading role.

4. With the exception of catastrophic health insurance, employers will play less of a role in determining what health care services can be purchased by their employees. Individuals will choose the services they desire, on the basis of information available on the Internet, for their day-to-day health care needs. Psychologists will have to aggressively market their services and provide consumers with information, via the Internet, that demonstrates the cost effectiveness of those services.

5. More employers will recognize the productivity benefit and cost-offset advantage to providing, in the workplace, programs to reduce stress, relieve symptoms such as depression, and promote psychologically and physically healthy lifestyles.

6. Psychology will continue to expand its scope of practice, particularly in the health care area. Most states will pass laws permitting appropriately trained psychologists to prescribe, and many psychologists will seek the necessary training at the postdoctoral level. Prescribing psychologists will become major participants in the health community and will help "open the doors" for other psychologists interested in applying their skills to health issues.

7. As more psychologists are drawn from other racial and ethnic groups, psychological services from psychologists of all kinds will become increasingly accepted, thus expanding the patient base and providing more assistance to populations that are currently underserved.

8. Psychologists will be in the vanguard of health professions utilizing technological advances from the Internet, telehealth, and other new developments.

9. Prospering as a health care psychologist will require flexibility, diversification of skills, an ability to adapt to changing economic and social conditions and a willingness to market aggressively and compete successfully with many other professions.

10. Psychologists in 2025 will be part of a truly international discipline in which the developments in one part of the world can be rapidly communicated to and implemented in other parts. Common standards for ethics, training, and practice will facilitate mobility and bring us together as a global profession.

Conclusion

Predicting the future is difficult and predicting the timing of changes is even more so. We believe that many of the trends we have identified will continue and will shape the future of professional psychology. Some may come much faster than anticipated, and others may lag behind, but most will happen. On balance, we believe these changes will be positive and will further the growth of professional psychology. If psychologists prepare themselves for the changes and embrace them, the next two decades could be the best in the history of professional psychology.

References

American Psychological Association. (1990). *Guidelines for providers of psychological services to ethnic, linguistic, and culturally diverse populations.* Washington, DC: Author.

American Psychological Association. (1995). *Task force on the changing gender composition of psychology: October 1995.* Retrieved February 6, 2006, from http://www.apa.org/pi/taskforce/

American Psychological Association. (2005) *Graduate study in psychology.* Washington, DC: Author.

Association of State and Provincial Psychology Boards. (2002). *Handbook of licensing and certification requirements for psychologists in the U.S. and Canada.* Montgomery, AL: Author.

DeLeon, P. H., Hagglund, K. J., Ragusea, S. A., & Sammons, M. T. (2003). Expanding roles for psychologists in the twenty-first century. In G. Stricker, T. A. Widiger, & I. B. Weiner (Eds.), *Handbook of psychology: Vol. 8. Clinical psychology* (pp. 551–568). New York: Wiley.

Gabel, J., Lo Sasso, T., & Rice, T. (2002, November 20). Consumer-driven health plans: Are they more than talk now? *Health Affairs,*

Web exclusive. Retrieved August 11, 2005, from http://content. healthaffairs.org/cgi/content/full/hlthaff.w2.395v1/DC1

Inouye, D. K. (1984, November). *Keynote address.* Presented at the 1984 annual convention of the Hawaii Psychological Association, Honolulu.

Kaiser Permanente. (2005, January). *The Medicaid program at a glance* (Fact Sheet No. 7235). San Diego, CA: Author.

Leong, F., Kohout, J., Smith, J., & Wicherski, M. (2003). A profile of ethnic minority psychology: A pipeline perspective. In G. Bernal, J. Trimble, & F. Leong (Eds.), *Handbook of racial and ethnic minority psychology* (pp. 76–77). Thousand Oaks, CA: Sage.

Levit, K., Smith, C., Cowan, C., Sensenig, A., Catlin, A., & Health Accounts Team. (2004). Health spending rebound continues in 2002. *Health Affairs, 23,* 147–159.

Mills, R., & Bhandari, S. (2003, September). *Health insurance coverage in the United States: 2002* (Current Population Rep. No. 60-223). Washington, DC: U.S. Census Bureau.

National Science Foundation. (2003). *Characteristics of doctoral scientists and engineers in the United States: 2001* (NSF Publication No. 03-310). Arlington, VA: Author.

National Science Foundation. (2004). *Doctoral scientists and engineers: 2001 profile tables* (NSF Publication No. 04-312). Arlington, VA: Author.

Newman, R., & Reed, G. M. (1997). Psychology as a health care profession: Its evolution and future directions. In R. J. Resnick & R. H. Rozensky (Eds.), *Health psychology through the life span: Practice and research opportunities* (pp. 11–26). Washington, DC: American Psychological Association.

Sax, L. J., Hurtado, S., Lindholm, J. A., Astin, A. W., Korn, W. S., & Mahoney, K. M. (2005, January). *The American freshman: National norms for fall 2004.* Los Angeles: Higher Education Research Institute, University of California at Los Angeles.

S. Rep. No. 108-81 at 7 (2003).

U.S. Government Accountability Office. (2005, May). *Report to the Chairman, Committee on the Budget, House of Representatives: Health information technology, HHS is taking steps to develop a national strategy* (GAO Publication No. 05-628). Washington, DC: Government Printing Office.

Thomas J. Vaughn

Epilogue:
For Students

Your education is the entire purpose of your professional program and your university. Your professors, internship supervisors, and postdoctoral supervisors have dedicated themselves to your training, mentoring, and ultimately to your success. They have invested their professional identities and their careers in you. Try to make them proud.

Your professional service to the public is the entire purpose that legislators had in mind when they chose to create licensure for psychologists. Those legislators respect the corpus of knowledge represented by your doctoral degree. They acted on behalf of the people, the people who need and expect you to provide competent and ethical services. Go do exactly that.

Appendix A:
Psychology Acronyms

AAAS: American Association for the Advancement of Science
AAP: Association for the Advancement of Psychology
AAP PLAN: Association for the Advancement of Psychology Psychologists for Legislative Action Now (PAC)
AAPI: APPIC Application for Psychology Internship
ABPP: American Board of Professional Psychology
ADA: Americans With Disabilities Act
ADAMHA: Alcohol, Drug Abuse, and Mental Health Administration
APA: American Psychological Association
ApA: American Psychiatric Association
APAGS: American Psychological Association of Graduate Students
APAIT: American Psychological Association Insurance Trust
APF: American Psychological Foundation
APAPO: American Psychological Association Practice Organization
APP: Association of Practicing Psychologists (APA-COR)
APPIC: Association of Psychology Postdoctoral and Internship Centers
APS: American Psychological Society
ASPPB: Association of State and Provincial Psychology Boards
ASPPBF: Association of State and Provincial Psychology Boards Foundation
AWP: Association for Women in Psychology

BAPPI: Board for the Advancement of Psychology in the Public Interest (APA)
BCA: Board of Convention Affairs (APA)
BEA: Board of Educational Affairs (APA)
BOD: Board of Directors

BPA: Board of Professional Affairs (APA)
BSA: Board of Scientific Affairs (APA)

CACES: Committee for the Approval of Continuing Education Sponsors (APA)
CAMP: Council of Applied Master's Programs in Psychology
CAPP: Committee for the Advancement of Professional Practice (APA)
CB: Credentials Bank (ASPPB)
CCOPP: Council of Credentialing Organizations in Professional Psychology
CE: Continuing Education; now CPE Continuing Professional Education (APA)
CEO: Chief Executive Officer
CFO: Chief Financial Officer
COO: Chief Operating Officer
CCPE: Committee on Continuing Professional Education (APA)
CERP: Committee for Examination Research and Policy (ASPPB)
CETOE: Committee on Education, Training and Oral Examinations (ASPPB)
CESPPA: Council of Executives for State and Provincial Psychological Associations (APA)
CIRP: Committee on International Relations in Psychology (APA)
CLGBC: Committee on Lesbian, Gay and Bisexual Concerns (APA)
CoA: Committee on Accreditation (APA)
CoS: Council of Specialties (APA)
COFA: Committee on the Future of the Association (ASPPB)
COGDOP: Council of Graduate Departments of Psychology
COLI: Committee on Legal Issues (APA)
COPA: Council on Postsecondary Accreditation
COPPS: Committee on Professional Practice and Standards (APA)
COR: Council of Representatives (APA)
CPA: Canadian Psychological Association
CPAP: Council of Provincial Associations of Psychologists
CPE: Continuing Professional Education (APA)
CPQ: Certificate of Professional Qualification in Psychology (ASPPB)
CPT: Current Procedural Terminology
CRHSPP: Canadian Register of Health Service Providers in Psychology
CRSPPP: Commission for the Recognition of Specialties and Proficiencies in Professional Psychology (APA)
CSFC: Committee on Structure and Function of Council (APA)
CWP: Committee on Women in Psychology (APA)

DLC: Division Leadership Conference (APA)
DoD: Department of Defense
DOT: Director of Training
DPA: Director of Professional Affairs
DSM: *Diagnostic and Statistical Manual*
DSM–TR: *Diagnostic and Statistical Manual—Text Revision*

EC: Executive Committee
ED: Education Directorate (APA)
EDC: Exam Development Committee (ASPPB)
EdD: Doctor of Education
ELC: Education Leadership Conference (APA)
EO: Executive Officer
EPPP: Examination for Professional Practice in Psychology
EFPA: European Federation of Psychologists' Associations
ETC: Committee on Education and Training for Credentialing (ASPPB)

FARB: Federation of Associations of Regulatory Boards
FPAC: Former Presidents' Advisory Council (ASPPB)

GC: General Counsel

HCFA: Health Care Financing Administration
HIPAA: Health Insurance Portability and Accountability Act
HIPDB: Healthcare Integrity and Protection Data Bank
HSA: Health Savings Account

IFC: Information for Candidates (ASPPB)
I/O: Industrial/Organizational (Psychology)

JCAHO: Joint Commission on the Accreditation of Healthcare Organizations
JCAHO–: Joint Commission on the Accreditation of Healthcare Organizations; MHC = Mental Health Care; PTAC = Professional and Technical Advisory Committee
JCEP: Joint Council on Professional Education in Psychology
JDC: Joint Designation Committee (ASPPB/NR)

MCE: Mandatory Continuing Education

NAMH: National Association of Mental Health
NAMI: National Alliance for the Mentally Ill
NAMP: Northamerican Association of Master's in Psychology

NASP: National Association of School Psychologists
NCSPP: National Council of Schools of Professional Psychology
NIH: National Institutes of Health
NIMH: National Institutes of Mental Health
NMS: National Matching Service (APPIC)
NPDB: National Practitioner Data Bank
NR: National Register of Health Service Providers in Psychology

ODEER: Office of Demographic Employment and Educational Research; now RO Research Office (APA)
OEMA: Office of Ethnic Minority Affairs (APA)

PAC: Political Action Committee (AAP PLAN)
P&C: Publications and Communications Board (APA)
P&P: Policy and Planning Board (APA)
PD: Practice Directorate (APA)
PDF: Psychology Defense Fund (APA)
PER: Psychology Executives Roundtable
PES: Professional Examination Service
PhD: Doctor of Philosophy
PO: Practice Organization (APA)
PPC: President's Planning Committee (ASPPB)
PsyD: Doctor of Psychology

RO: Research Office (APA)
RPC: Resource Planning Committee (ASPPB)

SAS: Sponsor Approval System (APA)
SD: Science Directorate (APA)
SIOP: Society for Industrial and Organizational Psychology, Division 14 (APA)
SLC: State Leadership Conference (APA)

TD: Training Director (APPIC)
TF: Task Force

VA: Veterans' Administration

WPO: Women's Programs Office (APA)

Appendix B:
Useful Web Sites

http://www.abpp.org: American Board of Professional Psychology

http://www.apa.org: American Psychological Association

http://www.apa.org/apags: American Psychological Association of Graduate Students

http://www.apapractice.org: American Psychological Association Practice Organization

http://www.appic.org: Association of Psychology Postdoctoral and Internship Centers

http://www.apait.org: American Psychological Association Insurance Trust

http://www.asppb.org: Association of State and Provincial Psychology Boards

http://www.crhspp.ca: Canadian Register of Health Service Providers in Psychology

http://www.cpa.ca: Canadian Psychological Association

http://www.nih.gov: National Institutes of Health

http://www.nimh.nih.gov: National Institute of Mental Health

http://www.nationalregister.org: National Register of Health Service Providers in Psychology

http://www.sba.gov: Small Business Administration

http://www.siop.org: Society for Industrial and Organizational Psychology

---

Note: Links to state and provincial association Web sites are available through http://www.apa.org.

Links to state and provincial licensing board Web sites are available through http://www.asppb.org.

Appendix C:
Credentials Recording Forms

ASPPB Association of State and Provincial Psychology Boards P. O. Box 241245 Montgomery, AL 36124 334-832-4580 www.asppb.org

APPLICATION TO DEPOSIT INFORMATION IN THE ASPPB CREDENTIALS BANK
PART B

Name: _____   File Number: _____

Information About Doctoral Degree Program

An official transcript must be submitted by all applicants directly to ASPPB by the institution granting the doctoral degree.

If coursework from another institution was applied toward your doctorate, a transcript must be provided from that institution (for example: masters degree transcript). If you completed respecialization training at another institution, submit official transcript from both the degree granting and respecialization training institutions.

Please provide information below about the institution granting the doctoral degree. Please provide information regarding applicable masters degree or respecialization in the table below.

Institution: _____

City: _____ State/Province: _____

Degree (circle one):   Ph. D.   Psy. D.   Ed. D.   Other: _____

Date Conferred: _____

Program of Study: _____ Clinical   _____ Counseling

_____ School   _____ Industrial/Organizational

_____ Other: _____ Specify: _____

Department: _____

Other Institution(s) Attended	Dates Attended	Full or Part Time?	Was coursework applied toward doctoral degree?

1. Was your doctoral degree obtained from an institution of higher education that was region- ☐ Yes   ☐ No
    ally accredited by an accrediting body recognized by the U.S. Department of Education or ☐ Don't Know
    authorized by Provincial Statute or Royal Charter to grant doctoral degrees at the time you
    received your degree?

2. Was your specific doctoral program accredited by the American Psychological Association ☐ Yes   ☐ No
    or the Canadian Psychological Association, or designated as a psychology program by the ☐ Don't Know
    National Register of Health Service Providers in Psychology and ASPPB at the time you
    received your degree?

ASPPB Association of State and Provincial Psychology Boards P. O. Box 241245 Montgomery, AL 36124 334-832-4580 www.asppb.org

3.   Was or did your doctoral program:

   a.   require three (3) years of full-time (or equivalent) graduate study, not including internship or postdoctoral supervised experience?   ☐ Yes   ☐ No

   b.   clearly identified and labeled as a psychology program (i.e., transcript, university catalog, etc.)?   ☐ Yes   ☐ No

   c.   an integrated, organized sequence of study?   ☐ Yes   ☐ No

   d.   include at least one year of full-time residency at the institution granting the doctoral degree (specify dates of full-time residency :_____)?   ☐ Yes   ☐ No

   e.   include an identifiable psychology faculty and a psychologist responsible for the program?   ☐ Yes   ☐ No

   f.   include supervised practicum, internship, field or laboratory training appropriate to the area of psychology practice?   ☐ Yes   ☐ No

Content Areas of Graduate Courses

Record appropriate graduate courses in the content areas listed below. Use the official course number and title; do not use abbreviations. Each course or portion of a course may be counted only once. **If a content area was covered in more than a single course or in a course with a title that is not indicative of that content, please provide supporting documents (e.g., a course syllabus or letter confirming coverage from the professor or the department chair).**

Scientific and Professional Ethics and Standards			
University	**Course Number**	**Course Title**	**Credit Hours**

Research Design and Methodology			
University	**Course Number**	**Course Title**	**Credit Hours**

Statistics and Psychometrics			
University	**Course Number**	**Course Title**	**Credit Hours**

ASPPB Association of State and Provincial Psychology Boards P. O. Box 241245 Montgomery, AL 36124 334-832-4580 www.asppb.org

Biological Bases of Behavior (e.g., physiological psychology; comparative psychology; neuropsychology; sensation and perception; psychopharmacology)			
University	Course Number	Course Title	Credit Hours

Cognitive-Affective Bases of Behavior (e.g., learning; thinking; motivation; emotion)			
University	Course Number	Course Title	Credit Hours

Social Bases of Behavior (e.g., social psychology; group processes; organization and systems theory)			
University	Course Number	Course Title	Credit Hours

Individual Differences (e.g., personality theory; human development; abnormal psychology)			
University	Course Number	Course Title	Credit Hours

Supervised Practical Experience in Rendering Psychological Services (e.g., practica, field work, internship, etc., as part of the doctoral program of studies)			
University	Course Number	Course Title	Credit Hours

I attest that the information contained in my responses to this form are true and correct to the best of my knowledge.

_____   _____
Signature   Date

ASPPB Association of State and Provincial Psychology Boards P.O. Box 241245 Montgomery, AL 36124-1245   334 832-4580 http://www.asppb.org

FORM 104

THIS FORM MAY BE SUBMITTED TO DOCUMENT COMPLETION OF A FORMAL PREDOCTORAL INTERNSHIP OR POSTDOCTORAL RESIDENCY PROGRAM AS A PORTION OF THE REQUIRED 2 YEARS/3,000 CLOCK HOURS OF SUPERVISED EXPERIENCE

Director of Predoctoral Internship or Postdoctoral Residency Verification Form
(duplicate if necessary)

Please Note: It is not acceptable to attach letters in lieu of completing this form.

See the instructions for Form 104 if person who actually directed internship/residency is not available to verify experience.

CPQ Applicant will complete this page and mail with the attached page to Reference:

Applicant Name: _____ Doctoral Degree: _____ Date: _____
Address: _____
City: _____ State: _____ Zip: _____ Telephone: _____
Applicant's title in the Internship/Residency _____
(e.g., Clinical Psychology Intern, Counseling Psychology Intern, School Psychology Intern)

Internship/Residency Agency _____
City: _____ State: _____ Zip: _____ Telephone: _____
How many interns/residents were in the program for the entire and same time you were? _____

Inclusive dates of internship/residency _____

Hours of Internship/Residency Supervision

Supervisor's Name (List primary first)	Supervisor's Degree (e.g., Ph.D., Psy.D., M.S., etc.)	Was Supervisor a Licensed Psychologist? Yes or No	Hours/week of Individual Supervision	Hours/Week of Group Supervision	Dates of Supervision From/To

Summary of Supervision Hour Totals

Total number of weeks worked excluding all leave?	
Average number of hours worked per week including supervision?	
Total number of hours worked during internship including supervision? (Weeks x hours per week = total hours)	
Total hours of **individual** supervision from all **licensed psychologists**?	
Total hours of **group** supervision from all **licensed psychologists**?	
Total hours of **individual** and **group** supervision from all **other licensed professionals**?	
Grand Total of hours of supervision during the internship/residency year?	

I declare that all of the foregoing is true and correct.

Signature of Applicant for CPQ   Date

ASPPB Use Only
CPQ File No. _____

Continued on Back

Form 104, pg. 1

Director of Predoctoral Internship or Postdoctoral Residency Verification Form

Former Intern/Resident:

Instructions to Supervisor completing this form:

The person (named above) is applying for a Certificate of Professional Qualification in Psychology (CPQ) issued by the ASPPB and has given your name as the director of his/her internship/residency program. Please review each page of this reference form and answer questions where indicated. Return the entire form to the CPQ Program at the address indicated below. If your responses need explanation, please provide appropriate comments on an attached sheet.

      Thank you for your time and effort.

ASPPB CPQ Program

What was the doctoral program area* of the Internship/Residency?

_____

*Area = Clinical, Counseling, School, Experimental, Social, etc.

Current Internship/Residency Program Director's Name: _____ Degree: _____

Are you licensed as a psychologist? _____ State(s)/Provinces _____

What is your area of doctoral specialty (e.g., Clinical, Counseling, School, etc.) _____

	Yes	No
Was the internship/residency APA approved when the applicant completed training?		
Is the information provided by the applicant correct? (If no, please explain in detail on an attached sheet)		
To the best of your knowledge does this person appear to have good moral character, and has he/she exhibited professional conduct at all times as defined by the Code of Ethics for Psychologists?		
To the best of your knowledge, did this person perform their duties as an intern/resident competently?		
To the best of your knowledge, did this person satisfactorily complete all aspects of the internship/residency program?		

If your answer to any of the above three questions is "No", please explain on an attached sheet.

_____

Signature of Director of Internship/Residency Program   Date

Please return this completed form to:	**CPQ Program**	**Telephone: (334) 832-4580**
	ASPPB	
	P.O. Box 241245	
	Montgomery, AL 36124-1245	

Form 104, pg. 2

ASPPB Association of State and Provincial Psychology Boards P.O. Box 241245 Montgomery, AL 36124-1245 334 832-4580 http://www.asppb.org

FORM 105

THIS FORM MAY BE SUBMITTED TO DOCUMENT SOME OR ALL OF THE REQUIRED 2 YEAR/3,000 HOURS OF SUPERVISED EXPERIENCE WHEN EITHER NO FORMAL PREDOCTORAL INTERNSHIP OR POSTDOCTORAL RESIDENCY WAS COMPLETED

VERIFICATION OF SUPERVISED EXPERIENCE FORM
PLEASE PRINT OR TYPE

Please Note: It is not acceptable to attach letters in lieu of completing this form.

Part I. - To be completed by the applicant for CPQ (Duplicate if necessary)

CPQ Applicant		
	NAME	
	CURRENT ADDRESS	
	CITY/STATE/ZIP	
	TELEPHONE #	
	Degree: Field:	

Former Supervisor		Degree	Licensed Psychologist
	NAME		☐ Yes ☐ No
	CURRENT ADDRESS		
	CITY/STATE/ZIP		

* See instructions for Form 105 if person who actually provided supervision is not available to verify this experience.

LOCATION(S)	List place(s) where you engaged in professional experience under this supervisor. If the place the actual supervision occurred is different, please clarify on a separate sheet of paper.	
		1	2
	LOCATION		
	ADDRESS		
	CITY/STATE		
	SUPERVISOR'S TITLE OR POSITION		
	SUPERVISEE'S TITLE OR POSITION		

DUTIES	Describe below, in detail, the training program and/or psychological duties performed while supervised.

# OF HOURS SUPERVISEE WORKED	DATES		Total Number of Weeks Worked	Number of Hours of Work per Week Including Supervision Provided	Total Number of Hours Worked During Entire Period Verified
	FROM MO/YR	TO MO/YR			

Form 105, pg. 1

Continued on Back

ASPPB Use Only
CPQ File No. _____

	TYPE OF SUPERVISION	HOURS PER WEEK OF SUPERVISION	SUPERVISOR(S) including person completing this form. For each additional supervisor listed, indicate degree and type of license held during period of supervision
SUPERVISION	INDIVIDUAL		
	GROUP		
	OTHER (SPECIFY)		
	TOTAL PER WEEK		

I declare that all of the foregoing in Part I of this form is true and correct.

_____
Signature of CPQ Applicant   Date

Part II - To be completed by supervisor named on page 1.

	YES	NO
Is the information provided by the former supervisee in Part I of this form accurate? If no, describe or discuss the differences on a separate sheet of paper and attach to this form.		
Were you (or the person who supervised this individual) engaged in rendering professional services at least 50% of the time in the same work setting in which the person supervised was obtaining supervised professional experience?		
Were you (or the person who supervised this individual) licensed to practice psychology or any other profession subjected to discipline by any state or country during the period of supervision? If yes, explain on a separate sheet of paper.		
Did you (or the person who supervised this individual) have a license on probationary status during the period of supervision? If yes, explain on a separate sheet of paper.		
Did you (or the person who supervised this individual) have a license in a delinquent status at any time during the period of supervision? If so, list the delinquent dates on a separate sheet of paper.		
Was the supervisee functioning in this same work setting under any other license or in any other professional capacity with the same client load during the period of supervision?		

I (or the person who supervised this individual) would rate the supervisee's performance during the period of supervision as: (check one)
☐ SATISFACTORY   ☐ UNSATISFACTORY

REMARKS: ASPPB would appreciate any amplifying information regarding your evaluation above.
_____

Please supply the following information about yourself:

Current Position or Title:_____
Degree: _____
Specialty Area (e.g., Clinical, Counseling, etc.):_____
License Number:_____ State/Province:_____ Issue Date:_____

I declare that all of the foregoing in Part II of this form is true and correct.

_____
Signature of Person Verifying Supervised Experience

_____
Date

_____
Telephone Number

Please return this completed form to:	**CPQ Program** **ASPPB** **P.O. Box 241245** **Montgomery, AL 36124-1245**	**Telephone: (334) 832-4580**

ASPPB Use Only
CPQ File No. _____

Form 105, pg. 2

Index

About the Editor

Thomas J. Vaughn, PhD, ABPP, has been in the private practice of behavioral medicine psychology for 24 years at a large multispecialty medical clinic and regional hospital in Shawnee, Oklahoma. In 1987 he became the first psychologist in Oklahoma to be granted full hospital privileges. He also serves as the psychological consultant to the Oklahoma Licensing Board, advising the board, doctoral program staff, students, and practicing psychologists on issues related to training, credentialing, professional practice, and ethical matters. He received his doctorate in counseling psychology from the University of Oklahoma, Norman, and has held a position as adjunct faculty at the university since 1990. He served for 18 years as the director of training for the Oklahoma Health Consortium Clinical Psychology Internship in Oklahoma City. He is a former president of the Association of State and Provincial Psychology Boards (ASPPB), a fellow of both the American Psychological Association and the ASPPB, and is board certified in clinical psychology by the American Board of Professional Psychology. Dedicated to solving the profession's mobility problem, Dr. Vaughn provided leadership in establishing mutual reciprocity agreements among and between U.S. states and Canadian provinces for mobility of licensure, which led to the development of the individual endorsement of licensure vehicle through the ASPPB Certificate of Professional Qualification in Psy-

chology. In response to a request from the American Psychological Association of Graduate Students for information
concerning licensure and certification for students, he developed a symposium on the topic that continues to be a popular
session at the convention of the American Psychological
Association.